"Many books on spirituality seem to aim too high and become inaccessible, while others merely reflect the current and passing language. Richard Gilmartin seems to have found the enduring wisdom that includes body and soul—without sacrificing True Transcendence. The Spirit speaks well here."

Richard Rohr, O.F.M.
Albuquerque, New Mexico

"This is a remarkable work, written with creative insight into the fundamental life task of facing humanness in order to find the spiritual. Dr. Gilmartin explores core life issues with clarity, depth, and conviction. He presents a comprehensive look at dealing with, not avoiding, the demands of psychological health as a vital foundation for spiritual ownership. He offers a freshness of perspective and a challenge to question truth until it becomes one's own.

Katie Kelley, Ph.D.
Grace Institute

"The holistic approach of *Pursuing Wellness, Finding Spirituality* is its strength. Dr. Gilmartin defines spirituality, the central motif of the work, as 'self-transcendence' that connects one with a transcendent being. He recognizes that both psychotherapy and religion have insights to offer, and that neither can ignore the importance of spirituality for the fully human person. The central questions of life and death, good and evil, freedom, aloneness, and meaningfulness are dealt with separately and at the same time in an integrated way. Spirituality, the heart of the book, is seen as 'arising out of deep personal experience' and out of community....The insights provided, the examples and case work described, will be good for all people in the 'healing professions,' those who work to heal the body, or the mind, or the soul. In accepting the integration of all three, the possibility for true healing of the person grows."

Sr. Catherine M. Harmer, M.M.S., Ph.D.
Psychologist and Author, *Religious Life in the 21st Century*

"Dr. Gilmartin's *Pursuing Wellness, Finding Spirituality* is about life as it is lived. Readers will likely find themselves reflecting on their own lives as they read. In the process they will find themselves understanding their everyday experiences, particularly seemingly negative ones, in a way that affirms and enlivens. The value of this book lies in the author's wisdom as a seasoned clinician and a person of faith."

Martin C. Helldorfer, D. Min.
Director of Education & Research
St. John Vianney Hospital, Downingtown, PA
Author, *The Work Trap: Rediscovering Leisure, Redefining Work*

"Throughout the world, men and women in leadership and various roles of responsibility are dramatically reshaping the way they think about wellness—physical, psychological, and spiritual. This book proposes a model for the interaction of the three realms that is clearer and more compelling than anything I have seen. Richard Gilmartin speaks to a profound and often profoundly neglected human need: personal ownership and responsibility for what each one can possibly become in life."

Joan Cronin, G.S.I.C.
Institute for Catholic Education
Toronto, Canada

"I finished reading Dr. Gilmartin's book on wellness in one sitting. I was so enthralled I just kept reading. It is a powerful book, one that contains images and stories, the effects of which are reminiscent of the teaching tales of the Hasidim. I believe anyone who is engaged in the quest for wellness of body, mind, and soul will find his reflections, stories, and images both informative and transformative.

"With a surgeon's skill and a mentor's presence, Dr. Gilmartin invites us to examine three fundamental modes of human presence (physical, psychological, and spiritual). In that process he gently shatters all those safe concepts we tend to hold about life, love, and relationships. And always he urges us to grapple with essential questions concerning good, evil, meaninglessness, aloneness, and death."

Thomas J. Tyrrell, Ph.D.
Author, *The Adventure of Intimacy:
A Journey through Broken Circles*

Pursuing Wellness, Finding Spirituality

RICHARD J. GILMARTIN

TWENTY-THIRD PUBLICATIONS

Mystic, CT 06355

Twenty-Third Publications
185 Willow Street
P.O. Box 180
Mystic, CT 06355
(860) 536-2611
800-321-0411

ISBN 0-89622-674-3
Library of Congress Catalog Card Number 95-61489
Printed in the U.S.A.

DEDICATION

To Nancy, my wife and life-mate, who has patience with my impatience, caring concern that persists in the face of my frequent preoccupations, and has never rationed her love or her companionship when life's crises threatened. Words could not contain what she means to me. It is to her that this book is dedicated.

FOREWORD

I am honored to introduce to you a book written by Dr. Richard Gilmartin, a leading psychotherapist at Southdown and a personal friend. Many years of working in psychotherapy and as a psychology professor have led Dr. Gilmartin to see that wellness is only possible if we become responsible for our own life and happiness. His new book sets out the steps required in the journey of becoming whole or well.

It is crucial that we know the art of intimacy and live an integrated emotional life. What happens to us when our sense of self is shame-based? How do we deal with stress and achieve a personal adulthood, and how do we cope with being vulnerable? Dr. Gilmartin maintains that wellness is only possible if we are well in our physical, psychological, and spiritual areas of life—much like a three-legged stool.

There has been much written in the past few years about physical and psychological healing and wellness. Dr. Gilmartin recognizes and treats the physical and the psychological, but he is much more interested and concerned about the spiritual. This component of the book makes it unique from other books written on the subject of wellness. It relates to the unheard cry for meaning that many experience in our age. It is this sense of spiritual wellness that is the significant focus of his work.

Each one of us is challenged with the task of developing a philosophy of life that gives meaning and purpose to our existence and that helps transcend the narrow self-interest of so much modern living. Many people today are simply surviving or "hanging in there." Many are caught up in a lifestyle of violence, addiction, dislocation, alienation, and loneliness. A new generation of seekers has arrived on the scene aware that the cellular phone, computer chip, and consumer goods, while helpful, do not provide meaningful living: The search is deeper and the yearning more profound.

Dr. Gilmartin invites us to face forthrightly the issues of life that lead to growth and true meaning. Some of these are death, suffering, freedom, aloneness, and meaninglessness. Yet, the single most important merit of Dr. Gilmartin's book on wellness is that it is based on lived experience. He is a man who has lived life and has journeyed with others in their search for meaning and wholeness. His unique ability to listen to others in their human struggle has given him a keen sense of the components of wellness. He knows what to say and write because he has been there.

I welcome this new work of Dr. Gilmartin and know that it will be a sure guide for many in their attempt to come to terms with life in a meaningful way as we come to the close of this, our twentieth century.

Paul E. Hansen, CSsR
Executive Secretary
International Justice and
Peace Commission (Redemptorist)
Rome, Italy

ACKNOWLEDGMENTS

The names of all those who have inspired thoughts in this book are too numerous to mention, but my gratitude to them lives in my heart. There are a few whose special contribution deserves mention. To Dennis Collins, colleague and friend, a special "thank you" for the time and effort given to reading and critiquing this manuscript. My gratitude to John and Paula Abraham who gave unstintingly of time and thought to this book's completion, and to Joan McMahon and Patty Roberts for their skill and time given to handling my often sloppy computer work. To J.A. Loftus and Donna Markham, the staff and residents of Southdown without whose presence in my life this book could not have been written, I offer my sincere appreciation.

Contents

PART III
SPIRITUAL WELLNESS

INTRODUCTION

It was his face that bore the signs of age—character, some might say. His body had a quasi-athletic look, young and vigorous, after 47 years of life. His face, however, looked like that of a 60-year-old, creased and weathered. His response to my query of "How can I help?" was to pin me with his tired, hard eyes and in a weary smoker's voice buttressed by a sigh say, "I'm a survivor, and I'm damn tired of it!"

As he said this, an image from a story told to me a few weeks prior came to mind. It was possibly more dramatic than the one of the man before me, but no less pained, yet with a different sense of liberation. The story was of a Roman Catholic monk in Lithuania who had been ordained in secret to serve the faithful of his Church. He had been hounded, arrested, imprisoned, tortured, and with the collapse of Soviet control in Eastern Europe, finally released after 18 years in prison.

After leaving the prison, the monk made his way to one of the houses of his order in Vilna, put on the religious habit which he had not worn in over 20 years, and with his head held high marched down the center of the downtown street to stand in front of KGB headquarters. Then, in a voice fired with the power to shake the headquarters to its foundations, he proclaimed, "I survived, you bastards, I survived!"

This story occurred behind the Iron Curtain, in a country that had been oppressed for over half a century, deprived of the freedoms that we in the West take for granted. The fact that the Lithuanian survived was a triumph for the human spirit, while the other man's survival felt more like defeat, humanness betrayed. After all, he was in North America, a place (at least for the United States and Canada) of wealth, unlimited opportunities, legal protection against discrimination, and the right to the pursuit of happiness. Why was my client's survival such a depressing exclamation? Why are we, a people who have so much, experiencing an epidemic of depression that makes this man not only not unique, but someone whom many of us can readily understand?

There are two kinds of survivors: those who survive the victimization of the powerful, and those who succumb to a self-inflicted, albeit unconscious, victimization. The former are our true heroes and heroines; their survival is a source of inner peace to them. Not only are their lives a source of inspiration for the rest of us, they possess a happiness only inner peace can give. The latter reflect the absence of that internal peace, displaying instead an inner deadness that robs them of happiness.

The man who sat with me in my office that day went on to talk about his "successes" in life. His work was steady, he made an adequate income, his dignity as a person was respected at work, his marriage was intact, and his three children were no significant worry for him. His health was of some concern, but mainly because stress was taking its toll. Although he would not have described himself as depressed, he clearly was, and without any identifiably specific trigger.

Given that the causes of depression are many and varied (some being underlying physical disorders), it is arguable that the majority of the approximately 35 million people in North America with a diagnosable clinical depression are depressed because of the way they are living their lives—or more correctly, the way they are *not* living their lives.

It is likely that these people are not even aware that they are depressed: Depression gets masked and shown only by symptoms, such as a lack of enthusiasm, nights of restless sleep, chronic boredom, pervasive tiredness, compulsive thrill-seeking, endless irritability, or seeing the high point of the day as the evening cocktail. For the man spoken of earlier, life has become an intolerable burden. The good news is that it does not have to be that way for him or for any of us.

There are certain common elements—call them needs, tasks, or processes—in a life well lived. If we fail to come to grips with these, we may suffer a gnawing sense of emptiness and failure. This, I believe, is a major contributor to depressive disease. Further, although life will offer opportunities to grapple with our inner selves, each of us bears the responsibility to take hold of these opportunities and use them to our benefit. This is the essence of wellness.

Our commitment to wellness must be total. If we commit to physical wellness, we must also commit to psychological and spiritual wellness. If one of these three elements is missing, we fail. Think of a three-legged stool. If one of the legs is broken, the stool is useless, no matter how strong the other two legs are.

This book will look at some of what we need to do with our physical selves if we are to practice wellness. Its main focus, however, is on exploring what makes for psychological and spiritual wellness. This is not a total or exhaustive exploration of all of our physical, psychological, and spiritual needs, only those that I perceive to be significant both within our Euro-American culture and at this time in history.

There are discussion questions at the end of each chapter. Use these for personal reflection, or talk them over with a friend or group of people. They are meant to challenge you to look at your life honestly and openly, and give you guides to probing the depths of your own unique lifestyle.

It is my hope that these ideas and suggestions for taking charge of our wellness will become a stimulus to self-exploration and perhaps, self-transformation.

PART I

PHYSICAL WELLNESS

CHAPTER 1

TAKING CARE OF OUR BODIES

Centuries from now, when historians reflect on the significant contributions made in the twentieth century, what has been done to lengthen human life expectancy may well dwarf the other discoveries made in this time. Over 30 years have been added to North American life expectancy in this century alone. This is a greater amount than was added in all the centuries up to the twentieth.

Additionally, not only are we living longer, we are also living younger longer. Perhaps you have had the experience, as I have, of looking back and thinking of your parents, school principal, or possibly a grandparent, and realizing that you are now the same age as they were then. You may think, "Wow! They seemed so old. . . I certainly don't *feel* that old!" Part of this is perspective, but there is also some truth there; they *were* "older" then than you are today.

Chronological age is rapidly becoming an unreliable measure of whether a person is young, middle-aged, old-aged, or elderly, the same way that mileage has become an unreliable measure of "how long it takes to get there." Some people are young at 50, others old at 40. Because of nutrition, exercise, and more knowledgeable health care, our bodies are not aging as fast as they did even 40 years ago. We are physically young for a longer period of time than our grandparents, parents, or even that school principal.

On the other hand, we are facing health hazards that previous generations did not face. Although we cannot do much (at present) about the most significant factor in our aging process —genes—there is a great deal we can do, not just to live longer, but to live more healthfully and youthfully. How we are living has a substantial effect on our physical wellness, how rapidly we age, and when and from what we will die.

You may be surprised to learn that the three leading "causes" of death in North America are not heart disease, cancer, and strokes. These are effects that are caused by something else. (A bullet in the brain may cause death, but the real cause of death is the person whose finger pulled the trigger.) The three leading causes of death in North America are diet, pollution, and stress.

The Center for Disease Control estimates that 50% of the U.S. mortality rate (and we have no reason to doubt that the same is true for Canada) is due to unhealthy behavior or lifestyles, and that 20% is due to environmental factors. What this means is that stress, poor diets, environmental pollutants, alcohol abuse, cigarette smoking, drug misuse, lack of exercise, failure to comply with medical advice, harmful social conditions, and inadequate health delivery systems are far more toxic than viruses and germs.

The message is clear: We must practice—and the key word here is practice—living in a way that respects our bodies, behaves responsibly towards them, says "no" to those things that can harm them, and "yes" to those things they need, and seeks the help of appropriate others when we are unable to carry through on our efforts. The rewards—inner peace, happiness, and a healthier life—far outweigh the difficulties we may encounter in practicing wellness.

On a basic level, to practice a healthy lifestyle one must stop smoking, be careful of alcohol use, eat sensibly, get adequate sleep, and engage in regular, health-appropriate exercise. (The Center for Disease Control also estimates that 12% of the U.S. mortality rate is directly connected to lack of exercise.) Newspapers, books, videos, magazines, and TV programs are full of advice concerning these issues, so there is no point repeating them here.

We live in an era that is supposedly health conscious, yet too many of us still do not do what needs to be done. What is needed are the will and the effort to practice a more healthy life style. Failures and slips are inevitable, but the more we keep at it, the better we get.

Retaining Our Youthfulness

Our capacity for healthy longevity is also related to our ability to maintain the characteristics of the young. We see this in adults who can still wonder, be excited, spontaneous and enthusiastic, invest themselves in doing or learning something new, and have fun for its own sake. They are living in the now, rather than running into the past or future. Above all, they have not lost—or they have re-acquired—the capacity to play.

Play, by definition, is purposeless activity; work, its opposite, is always purposeful. Children play naturally. For example, they run with no purpose other than the sheer pleasure of it. Adults run, and measure their pulse to bring it to a certain level, or try to run a predetermined distance in a certain time. Usually we play golf to achieve a certain score, beat a partner, or gamble on the outcome. Some of us even take a vacation only for the purpose of getting back to work with renewed energy. There is nothing wrong with any of this, but it is not really play.

To truly play we should do something just for the doing, like juggling, putting together a jigsaw puzzle, going to an amusement park (take a child along if you need justification), roaming the streets, sledding, skating, walking, running, swimming—anything, as long it has no extrinsic purpose. Above all, do not schedule in play for "X" amount of time each day: Do it spontaneously. Not only does this keep us young, but it may save our lives.

Another important issue in practicing physical wellness is the feeling that we are "carrying our weight," doing something that is useful and valued by others, making a contribution. Many of us find this in our work, in what we do to sustain our families or communities, or in donating our time and effort to worthwhile causes or activities. This need to be valued and useful is so critical to our well-being that often our work becomes the way we define ourselves.

Even though our understanding of this may change over time, a person's need to feel herself or himself as one who is valued, useful, and contributing does not change. In our society, this is especially problematic for the aged. We are a culture that overvalues youth and devalues those beyond a certain age, resulting in a perception that people are less valuable or useful as they age. We tend to shelve our elderly, and sentence them to "lives of leisure" with the implicit message that they have nothing more to contribute. It is little wonder that depression and suicide are significant health issues with the elderly.

This issue may become increasingly important during the next century as our technical knowledge explodes exponentially, thereby rendering the training and expertise necessary in many fields today obsolete. This, along with economic conditions such as downsizing, restructuring, and the like, will force many people into effectively retiring at an earlier age than may have been planned for and anticipated. There will be increasing pressure on governments to address these issues as the number of those in the final third of life increases and they are unwilling to simply wait idly for death. In the meantime what can we do to protect ourselves against potential marginalization?

There is much we can do. Although the earlier we start preparing for old age the better, it is never too late. We can keep active, enriching our lives with what we find fulfilling. We can keep learning, not only within our professions, but in new areas, recognizing that the true professional is a life-involved person, and not just a job-involved one. We must see ourselves as perpetual students, keeping active intellectually and searching for ways to make a contribution to others. The greatest danger we face is to disengage from life and surrender to aging. This is not only debilitating, but also invites disease and death into our life, displacing the life-giving forces.

Most of what happens to us physically is within our control. Of course, death is inevitable; but there is too much in life to be experienced and enjoyed before the inevitable actually occurs. How well we live up to that moment is not only our responsibility, but a God-given privilege and joy.

Questions for Discussion

1. What is your attitude toward your own body? Do you take pride in it and feel at home in it? Or are you ashamed of it, feeling like you would move out if you had a choice? How do you show pride in it, or how do you show shame?

2. Does play have a regular place in your life? Do you need an excuse to let yourself play and enjoy it? Do you have enough self-confidence to play with gusto?

3. In what ways does your being alive have a significant effect on others? Who are those people whose existence has a significant effect on you? Is life, for you, a process of achievement or a process of enjoyment? Can you blend these two processes together? How?

4. If you really had your druthers, and were not saddled with economic responsibilities, what would you do for and with the rest of your life? Why do you think you could not do this right now? Is this a realistic fear, or an avoidance?

PART II

PSYCHOLOGICAL WELLNESS

CHAPTER 2

RELATIONSHIPS

One of the basic principles of psychology is repeated so often it has become a cliché: "Good interpersonal relationships are the most effective prophylactic against mental illness." I am convinced that this is true—good friends *are* the best defense we have against being debilitated by emotional problems. However, I would take this a step further. Not only are intimate relationships essential for emotional stability, being intimate with people of both sexes is *necessary* if we are to fully develop as human beings.

Men and women each touch different facets in us that permit a different self to emerge. Of course, eventually these blend into a single self, but if all our close relationships are with one sex, then our personalities get warped. Witness the confirmed bachelor or spinster who avoids contact with the other sex, and how their personality is affected. The healthiest people I meet are those who have intimate relations with people of both sexes; this does not imply that they are involved in a sexual relationship with both (or either) sex. Actually, intimacy has little to do with sex, other than the fact that it can enhance it. We can have sex within, or without, intimacy, most finding it better within; this implies that there already is an intimacy which the sex expresses and expands.

None of the above is likely new to you. To say that intimacy is necessary for us, even intimacy with both sexes, is something most are well aware of. There is a deeper question, however: What is intimacy, and how do we achieve and sustain it without compromising our integrity? To answer this, we will look at the nature of intimacy, its various types, and the blocks to its formation. But first, let's look at a related issue.

Loneliness

When we lack intimacy, we become aware of a chronic, gnawing loneliness that affects every aspect of our lives. But it would be a mistake to attribute all feelings of loneliness to a lack of intimacy. We can have intense, intimate relationships and still be lonely.

So, what is loneliness? Like Louis Armstrong's response to the question "What is jazz?" ("Man, if you gotta ask, I can't tell you; you just know it!"), we just know what loneliness is because we have experienced it. It is a sense of being cut off, of not belonging, of having no one to relate to. It comes in many guises, like the loneliness we experience when we have been rejected by someone significant, or when there is no one who is important in our lives. There is the loneliness that comes when we are in the grip of a depression, the feeling that life is a blur and we are in unyielding darkness. There is the loneliness of being made to feel unacceptable because of race, sex, sexual orientation, age, nationality, religion, personality, or economic condition.

Loneliness is found in the adolescent who is struggling to find an identity and self-worth. In a similar place is the middle-aged person who questions the significance of his or her life, and seeks a new identity and source of value. There is the loneliness of illness and suffering, of the recently divorced, the alienated, and those who, for economic reasons, are on the edge of society. There is the loneliness of the person who feels that his or her life is meaningless and purposeless, of the abused child, of those who are made to feel that their feelings are unacceptable, or those who are not allowed to feel. There is the loneliness of facing our imminent mortality, of feeling misunderstood and condemned, of being fired.

Whatever its source, loneliness is a painful human experience. In some ways it is like pain itself: not something most people seek, but also not an enemy to be avoided at all costs. Without pain, our life would be a short one. It serves as a signal warning us that something is awry; we need to pay attention, discover what it is, and do something about it. Because pain can be so noxious, we are impelled to do whatever is needed to make it stop. Yet we also have the option of enduring pain for the sake of some higher value or goal, and thus achieve a transcendence that would not be possible if one chooses simply to end the pain.

The same is true for loneliness. It, too, serves as a signal that something is awry in our life and we need to address it before more serious damage is done to our psyche. Yet we may choose to endure the pain of loneliness for the sake of some value or goal that leads to greater maturation.

What, then, is loneliness? First of all, it is not the same as solitude, as "being alone." Most of us need to be alone from time to time; if deprived of this we can feel a self-alienation akin to loneliness. Solitude offers time to reconnect with our inner self. It is a time to recenter and refocus, to be sure we are coming to the world from our own inner being, *responding* to the external world, rather than reacting to it.

When we feel frazzled by demands on us, besieged by people wanting our time, energy, and thoughts, we need to pull inward and shut out the world. One of the reasons why meditation is so helpful in reducing stress is that it provides an inner space where we are free of the "world-out-there." This is also why people make retreats, take long walks on the beach, and cry for a time-out; without moments of solitude, we get painfully lonely.

Yet solitude can be difficult to find in our society. There is so much going on around us that finding the space and time to be alone and in touch with the internal is not easy to come by. For many people, there are only two places where they can find solitude: One is in the bathroom (even then, there may be someone pounding on the door telling us to "Hurry up!"), and the other is in the car.

Cars are the modern equivalent of the monastic cell, a place where we can go and be cut off from the external world. We do not relate to those cars around us, (except to avoid them), but stay in our own cocoon of solitude, thinking, fantasizing, planning, or simply flushing out the worries of the workaday world. This may be the reason why there is so much resistance to car pooling, even though it would significantly reduce worrisome pollution: We would then lose one of the few places of solitude and anonymity still left to us.

It is unfortunate that we often use solitude as a form of

punishment—we sentence prisoners to solitary confinement, suspend the misbehaving student from class, and send the recalcitrant adolescent to her room. We confuse isolation with solitude. Isolation is painful, but solitude is essential to being able to live authentically.

To further illustrate that loneliness and being alone are not synonymous, witness that we often experience the most painful loneliness in crowded places. Bars, classrooms, and shopping centers are full of lonely people becoming aware that physical proximity does not overcome the sense of isolation.

We are by nature social animals, in spite of our need for solitude. The bonding instinct is basic to us, and our survival depends on it. We bond first to our mothers, then to a family, then to larger groups and organizations such as schools, religions, racial and national groups, or geographical spaces. Later in life we bond to work or occupational groups, sexual partners, new families, and a wide variety of special interest groups. We do not survive long cut off from the groups that define and nurture us. They become an integral part of how we see ourselves and how others see us.

Answer the question: "Who am I?" Notice how many of the self-descriptive statements we may use imply being part of a group (or, possibly, not being part of a group). We may answer by saying, "A psychologist, a parent, a husband, a Caucasian, an alumnus, a Christian, an American, Irish" . . . and so on. All of these imply a bondedness with someone or something, a belonging to a larger group or network of others. It is only after exhausting our more communal responses that we may describe ourselves in more individual ways, such as kind, gentle, jealous, vain, empathic, abrasive, and so on.

We are safest (and feel most secure) within our own tribe

(however you constitute it), and most at risk outside it. This is the feeling of "at-one-ness" we get when we are in our own neighborhood, bed, or country, or with relatives, members of our church, age group, and the like. This is also why going on vacation can cause stress, as we leave the familiar and travel to unfamiliar places.

The instinctive drive to be safe may have been more needed in the period of history when all humans lived in the jungle or on the plains, and less necessary in more "advanced" civilizations. But our basic instincts are still primitive and prepare us for life "in the wild," more than for a modern, North American village. This is important to remember and will come up again as we look at instincts such as anger, sexuality, and stress.

Four Areas of Connectedness

There are four kinds of connections that keep us from being lonely. If one of these is missing in our lives, it can cause loneliness. When more than one connection is missing or broken, however, the pain of loneliness can be overwhelming and can move from being a stressful situation to a full-blown depression. It is important that if one connection is broken in our lives, we be sure the other three are strong. Also, when we feel lonely, it is important to identify where the connection has been broken, lest we put energy toward trying to end the loneliness in the wrong place.

The first connection is a *transcendent*, or cosmic, one. We need to feel connected to something larger than ourselves, to know that our life has a meaning and significance that transcends our own boundaries of space and time. For many, this connection is to a supernatural entity: God, Shiva, the Great Spirit, Nature. It could be to a cause, such as the green movement, the pro-choice or the pro-life movement, achieving world peace, keeping in harmonious balance with nature, or any similar involvement that helps us see ourselves as having a self-transcendent purpose.

It is not enough, however, to simply have a transcendent connection: We must also feel that we are living in harmony with it. Some years ago I was working with a woman who was president of her local pro-life group. Not only did she sincerely believe in the pro-life position, she was dedicated to it, committing much time and energy to promoting it. This involvement gave her life meaning, purpose, and value, while partly compensating for her less-than-satisfying marriage.

This upbeat, optimistic, life-affirming woman went into an acute depressive reaction when her unmarried, 16-year-old daughter got pregnant, and she procured an abortion for her. In a therapeutic setting, she could talk about guilt, for there was much there; but there was also a profound sense of having betrayed something essential to her selfhood. She had compromised her life's transcendent meaning, and the deep loneliness all but devastated her. When we are unfaithful to that which we believe about the world and the response that belief expects of us, we sever a connection of bondedness, and thereby experience loneliness.

A second connection affecting loneliness is a *cultural* one. Each of us is born into a culture, and it becomes an inherent part of us. This not only helps define who we are, it also shapes how we view the world and provides a sense of "at-homeness" with those with whom we share this culture.

Culture is a constellation of norms, values, foundational concepts, beliefs, behaviors, attitudes, and preferences. Positively, culture gives us a solid sense of identity, which includes a sense of both "who we are" and "who we are not."

We need this identity if we are to live effectively. Yet the negative aspect is that cultures tend to devalue the "who we are not" in order to feel positive about "who we are." As destructive as this prejudice is, it seems to be anthropologically natural to humans.

Since instilling a culture is, to a large extent, done unconsciously and reflexively, what we need to do is to make a conscious effort to not devalue other cultures as we learn to value our own. Although in the primitive stages of human existence fear of "the different" served to protect, this condition is no longer needed. Parents, teachers, religious leaders, and governmental officials all need to make a deliberate attempt to alter the tendency to see one culture as "better than" and another as "less than." This reeducation is essential if we are to live harmoniously in a multicultured world.

When we move into a different culture, especially one that is radically different from our own, we experience a loneliness even if there are strong interpersonal ties within the new culture. This loneliness is what impelled immigrants to North America, especially in the nineteenth and twentieth centuries, toward ghettos, ethnic neighborhoods, and ethnically based social and religious organizations. Accordingly, much of the strength of the religions in North America rested on cultural, rather than creedal, foundations.

Changes, or even the threat thereof, brought on by such events as different cultures moving into a neighborhood, a minority's movement toward full equality, or the flaunting of cultural norms by adolescents or dissidents can evoke a severe reaction on the part of members of the dominant culture. Movements that threaten norms—such as the women's movement, liberal religious movements, or anarchistic movements—evoke strong defensive reactions that are intended to protect the cultural psyche. Our identity, our psychic home-ostasis if you will, is threatened; if our culture gets destroyed, we become "displaced persons."

This is not intended as an argument for the *status quo* or for protectionism from movements pressing for full equality for all members of society. Rather, it is an attempt to work toward justice from a position of understanding. Nature is concerned with our survival (and that of the species) and the tribal para-digm has best served this. Yet monoculturism is no longer viable for most of the world, as populations grow, means of transportation become more efficient, and economic opportu-nities shift. Multiculturalism is the new reality. Eventually, new cultures arise out of the blends and shifts that may be sta-ble enough to sustain a sense of belonging.

The third connection to loneliness is *social*. Besides being born into a particular culture, we also become part of a social network which gives us a value and a sense of belonging. All societies are hierarchical; there are upper classes, lower class-es, and in some cases, middle classes. Hierarchies exist in all professions, groups, and institutions: seniors and juniors, the experienced and the inexperienced, the "ins" and the "outs." Sometimes hierarchies are rigid, birth-determined, cast in stone; at other times they are more flexible, with movement occurring up and down the scale determined by a variety of criteria—education, money, athletic ability, physical attractive-ness, and the like. Whether fixed or flexible, they are hierar-chies nonetheless, and people are generally conscious of where they fit in.

Social loneliness arises whenever we feel on the fringes of society. (A "society" can be a country, state, province, or the smaller "society" of a family, workplace, church, school, or neighborhood.) Those that the society sees as unacceptable because of race, nationality, age, sex, physical qualities or limitations, disease, or economic condition can all experience loneliness. We feel this way when we are fired from a job, get rejected by an institution or group that we valued belonging to, or are judged to be a failure.

Those whom society looks down on, judges to be deviant, or sees as a burden also experience social loneliness. Within a family it hits those who are seen as the black sheep, the scapegoat, or the "identified problem member." It is little wonder that those who feel alienated by society tend to band together with other "victims" of society to form a new social group within which they can gain acceptance and compensate for feelings of insignificance.

The fourth connection, and the one that all of us are most familiar with, is the interpersonal one. Loneliness can arise whenever we are separated from or lose someone in our life to whom we have significant emotional ties. It can hit suddenly as a result of death, rejection, or abandonment. It may also be a chronic, lingering emptiness because we lack a significant connection to another person, when there is no one in life with whom we are truly intimate.

There are two types of loneliness akin to this interpersonal one, which are related, but differently treated. Intrapersonal loneliness arises when we disown pieces of ourselves, be this our anger, our sexuality, our jealousy, our race, or any other significant portion of us. Self-disowning is self-alienating; the result is that we do not feel fully at home with who and what we are.

There is also an existential kind of loneliness. No matter how intense and complete our intimate connections are, there is a part of each and every one of us that will never be touched by another. Deep in our being is a place known only to us and essentially unshareable with another. Sometimes, in solitary moments, we touch this space and feel the isolation. As much as we would like to be totally known and accepted by another, it is not possible. Existential loneliness can be foundational to our spirituality, and I will address it when we come to that part of the book.

Before we move further into the interpersonal dimension, let us revisit our overall understanding of loneliness. I hope we have arrived at the understanding that loneliness is not an illness requiring treatment, or symptomatic of mental illness, or indicative of personal failure. It is a healthy reflex that calls for an honest recognition of the loss of someone or something meaningful to us, be that a relationship with God, a purposeful life, a cultural connection, a place in society, or a loved one. It may also signal our need for companionship and love, for touching base with our roots, for deciding how to respond to a society that may alienate us.

As we grow from honestly coping with the source of our loneliness, we may find ennoblement in choosing to break one of our connections. Although this can truly be a source of pain, it need not be feared, for the fear of loneliness can be more disabling than loneliness itself.

We may walk away from someone or something which gives meaning to our existence in order to move into deeper spiritual growth; we may sever ties to our culture and move into a different one in order to provide our family or children with greater opportunity; we may choose to become an outcast within our social group in the service of justice; we may leave those we love in the service of love. If we do take any one of these steps and thereby incur the inevitable loneliness, however, it behooves us to keep the other three connections as strong as possible for the sake of our well-being.

Intimacy

Most of us long to connect with another in a fully intimate way, even though we resist doing what we need to in order to achieve it. The amount of social involvement we need may vary, and our desire for privacy may increase as we age, but our need for intimacy itself is a constant. This is true for the sexually promiscuous, the celibate monk, the happily married, or the single person.

Although there is intense bonding in infancy and strong attachments in childhood and adolescence, true intimacy does not seem to appear until adulthood. We need a certain security in who we are, before we can let someone else get close to us, without it threatening our own identity. The fear of being absorbed by the other may be too great before our sense of autonomy is secure.

Most people find intimacy within their friendships. Obviously, not all our friendships will be intimate ones; in fact, non-intimate friendships will far outnumber the intimate ones, and rightly so. Although there are many kinds of friendships, they can realistically be reduced to two: social friendships and intimate friendships. The former are those people we work with, go to school with, live near, belong to clubs with, have a drink with, tell a joke to, do a favor for, and so on. We share time with these people but generally do not share too much of ourselves. We enjoy their company, and they add something important to our lives. Yet as valuable as these friendships are, we need more than these kinds of friends.

A Roman Catholic priest, a pastor of a well-to-do urban parish, a talented, attractive, respected man, once said to me: "You know, in my parish there are 45 families whose homes I could go to for dinner on any Sunday afternoon. I'd be welcomed there, made to feel part of the family, and have a great time. The thing is, however, none of them would miss me if I didn't come." Although this priest was a highly regarded man with a large number of friends, he had no one with whom he was intimate. His celibate commitment actually facilitated his social friendships, but, at least in his perception, it hindered forming intimate ones.

Let me pose a question for you. When your alarm clock goes off tomorrow morning, who cares if you are still breathing? I mean, who *really* cares? Sure, there will be many who care because they are affected or inconvenienced by your death—the person who has to cover your work, those who depended on you for some aspect of their own life, whomever has to straighten out all the loose ends you leave behind. But who *really cares* about you? It may come as a surprise how often people answer this question with: "No one!"

Let me pose a second, more important, question. Whom do *you* care that, when their alarm clock goes off, they are breathing? Who do you miss when they are not there? Not to be loved is sad, but not to love is tragic. We cannot do much about making other people love us; that is beyond our control. But we can be people who love; this is within our control. We cannot force an intimate relationship to happen, but we can be open to the possibility of one, so that when the moment occurs we are ready to respond.

What is intimacy? A clue to its meaning can be found in the word itself. The root of the word is the Latin verb *intimare* which literally means "to bring or put inside." In a sexual relationship this happens physically, but it is misleading to make "being intimate" synonymous with having sexual intercourse. True intimacy is a psychological entering inside the other, and permitting the other to enter inside us. Having a sexual relationship with another does not, in itself, bring intimacy; witness the number of married couples who, presumably, have a sexual relationship but do not have an intimate relationship in the sense of feeling at one with each other.

Sex is a way of expressing intimacy, never a way of achieving it. Too often, we enter into a sexual relationship with another when what we really want is intimacy. We can then find ourselves feeling empty, perhaps mildly depressed, wanting to put some space between ourselves and our partner. Sex can be intensely pleasurable, while intimacy is deeply satisfying. Whenever we separate sex from love, love suffers, and consequently our desire for true intimacy is never really fulfilled.

To permit another to psychologically enter inside us is to put aside the masks, pretenses, phoniness, lies—all the things about our self that we create in order to appear admirable—and permit the other to see us as we are, warts and all. This is the primary, indispensable condition for an intimate relationship to occur. Obviously, we are vulnerable when we do this. We open ourselves to rejection, humiliation, even exploitation, but also to the possibility that we will no longer be alone. No one consciously chooses to be vulnerable; it is too frightening. We would all choose to "be strong," invulnerable. But this is an unrealistic wish.

Not only are we highly vulnerable (and any invulnerability illusory), the attempt to be invulnerable prevents us from achieving what is most valued in life. Too many of us pursue admiration when what we really want is love. We can admire a statue, a person of great talent and accomplishment, another's intellect or athletic prowess, but we can only love a human being, with all his or her imperfections, and this requires knowing that person's truth.

Love has the power to heal and transform, but this cannot

take place unless we feel the other's love for us. If we have kept aspects of ourselves hidden, and another says to us, "I love you," our response may be "Yes, but. . .if you really knew me you wouldn't!" In this state, the love given simply runs off us, rather than cleansing our wounds. But, if we have permitted another to see those aspects of us that we are most ashamed of—as well as those that we are most proud of—and the other says "I love you," then we can hear it, let it touch us, and interiorize it. This is the love that transforms.

So, the first condition necessary for intimacy is our willingness to let another know us as authentically as possible. The second is that the other receive us in a non-judgmental way. Obviously, if the other criticizes, condemns, or rejects, then our sharing stops, the relationship freezes, and we pull back from intimacy. We have to feel acceptance from the other to continue on in an intimate relationship. This does not mean total approval, but is akin to the "unconditional positive regard" that noted psychologist Carl Rogers lays down as critical for the success of psychotherapy. For intimacy to occur, there has to be a feeling of acceptance as we are, without an attempt to reform or correct.

The third condition of intimacy is that the relationship be mutual. As we share ourselves, we are trying to know you, and the other, and he or she must try to share who they are with us. We are not competitors—that would be destructive to intimacy—but two people acting within a reciprocal relationship. If we are only interested in others knowing us, it is narcissism; if we are only interested in knowing others, without them knowing us, it is voyeurism. Neither of these states leads to intimacy; mutuality must be present.

Eight Types of Intimacy
There are eight different types of intimacy that correspond to

people's different needs; no one person would ever be able to meet them all for any of us. Thus, although we cannot tolerate a large number of intimate friends, for reasons we will see shortly, we do need more than one.

All of us have moments when a spark of intimacy gets ignited. If we choose to pursue it, there is a likelihood that an intimate relationship can be built; if we ignore it, either through choice or circumstance, the spark cools and nothing continues beyond the moment. How this happens will become clearer as each type of intimacy is described.

First of all, there is an *emotional intimacy*. This occurs when we are able to share a feeling with another and sense that the other understands perfectly what we are describing. It also happens when someone expresses a feeling that we know, but cannot describe. This sometimes occurs in therapy groups, especially sensitivity-type groups. Here someone may express a feeling that we, too, recognize and have felt. At that moment there exists a oneness between us; we know that here is a kindred soul.

There is also an *intellectual intimacy*, where we are able to share ideas with another and feel understood. This is similar to emotional intimacy, in that someone expresses a thought that we, too, have had but may not have been able to express. Another kindred soul who thinks as we do communicates their understanding of *ideas* that we are trying to communicate. The sense of at-one-ness is in the expression of thought.

Next is an *aesthetic intimacy*, when we share something beautiful with another. Perhaps you are walking with someone on a crisp autumn afternoon when you both become aware of a magnificent sunset that fills the sky with glorious color. You both stop and look. There is no need for words, you simply share the beauty. At that moment a barrier breaks and, in a real sense, you merge with another. Perhaps you have had the reverse experience where you come upon something beautiful—a painting, a play, a piece of music—and wish that a particular person was there to share it with you. Not only would they enjoy it, but your own enjoyment would be enhanced by theirs.

Creative intimacy happens when we are able to work well with another, to make something happen together that does not happen alone. When working with this person, we are like two gears in the same machine, functioning smoothly and facilitating each other's effort. This happens with basketball, football, and hockey teams when two players click, and each makes the other better. There is an intimacy between them that may not carry over into other situations, but as long as they are working (or playing) together they are at one.

Recreational intimacy comes when we can laugh with another. This occurs when we are with someone whose company we simply enjoy; we have fun with this person without any of the strain of having to keep the conversation going, or searching for what to say next. The relationship is effortless.

There is a *crisis intimacy* when two people share a transformative, frequently tragic incident and are drawn into a oneness. The parents of a child killed in a traffic accident feel this horror together and are drawn into a bond of shared grief. In this tragedy, they are at one with the intimacy that a crisis creates.

Erotic intimacy happens when the other person touches something inside us that results in an urgent longing to be sexually intimate with her or him. It is different than merely finding someone sexually attractive, or even being "turned-on" by someone; it is a desire to possess the other totally—physically, sexually, permanently. When it is mutual and expressed, we feel an at-one-ness with a passion we hope will never end.

Finally, there is *spiritual intimacy*, where we can share our deepest beliefs about life, death, immortality, evil, soul. Sometimes we meet a kindred spirit with whom we can bare our souls. Therapists often achieve this for others, and their clients get an illusion of intimacy. But for real spiritual intimacy to occur the relationship must be mutual, and this should never occur in a therapeutic setting.

Historically, some of the greatest love relationships appear to be of spiritual intimacy: Abelard and Eloise, Francis of Assisi and Clare, Benedict and Scholastica, Nicholas and Alexandra, Elizabeth Cady Stanton and Susan B. Anthony to name a few. Where there is an in-depth and mutual soul-sharing, we achieve a spiritual at-one-ness.

The Role of Intimacy

A friend is one with whom we can share on one or more of these dimensions. The more significant, and possessing, the relationship is, the more the number of intimacies we share. Marriage, for example, is a multidimensional relationship. Most likely erotic intimacy is there; however, unless some of the other intimacies, like emotional, intellectual, or spiritual, are present, the relationship wears out, becoming boring and burdensome. The erotic alone is never enough to sustain as significant a relationship as the married one.

There is wisdom in the old caution about jumping into marriage precipitously. The erotic can cloud perception and judgment so that we may overlook the other kinds of intimacy necessary to sustain what all of us hope is a lifelong committment. This will become even more important in years to come, as culturally, marriage increasingly relies on the emotional support two people give to each other, while economic dependence becomes less a felt need.

When we look at the eight types of intimacy, we can learn much about the nature of intimacy. Although it would be nice to have relationships in each area, only some are essential. The emotional and intellectual, it would seem to me, are indispensable; it would be hard to go through life without someone to share thoughts and feelings with, feeling not understood and accepted. The aesthetic, creative, and recreational significantly enhance life, but although our enjoyment of life's beauty would be diminished, and work and leisure less life-giving, we could live without these.

Crises are easier to bear with another in the same emotional space, but this kind of intimacy is fraught with danger. The same intimacy that helps us bond and survive the crises can block us from dealing with the anger, blaming, and guilt that pass between two people coping with a tragedy. If these remain unarticulated, they poison and can ultimately destroy the relationship: Witness how many marriages cannot survive the death of a child.

Erotic intimacy is important for most of us, but many survive quite well without it. This area, too, can be dangerous; we all experience some attractions that can be potentially harmful. Often, we resist erotic intimacy because it can threaten other intimacies that we treasure.

Most people reach out for others to walk the spiritual journey with; religious organizations survive on this need and, in the Judeo-Christian tradition, authentic spirituality is found only in community. When we fail to find a soul mate, someone with whom we can reflect on our unique spiritual journey, the tendency to rely on communal norms often leads to mediocrity. Ultimately, we must rely on our own intuition, but the presence of another with whom we share our inner voices is invaluable.

Again, no one person will ever be able to meet all our intimacy needs and wishes. Accordingly, we must relinquish the search for one who will totally meet our needs in order to really experience what intimacy we can achieve. Our mothers come closest to being the other who is totally dedicated to our well-being and who can meet all needs. Yet we only get one mother, and she comes early in our life.

The search for Prince Charming or the Fair Maiden—the "other" who will come and sweep us up into a bliss-filled existence—is doomed to frustration. Myths may embody universal longings, but we are limited to flesh-and-blood realities, persons with whom we can build mutual relationships wherein intimacy will be created.

We all need several intimate relationships in our lives, with both sexes, in order to meet the variety of intimacies. On the other hand, we have to protect ourselves against too many intimate relationships, else we lose too much self-sufficiency.

We cannot take someone by the hand and say "Let's go out for a walk to see the sunset and have an intimate moment together!" Intimate moments simply happen (and they likely happen often), and we may or may not respond to them. We may choose not to respond because there simply is not space in our life for another such relationship; this need not diminish our enjoyment of the moment. If we choose to sustain that relationship, we have to work at it.

Intimate relationships take time and effort. When we are involved in such a relationship, the other person has a right to expect time together, effort to make contact when distance or circumstances separate you, and consideration when there are life choices to be made that could affect your relationship. A loss of freedom arises with intimate relationships because we must now live our lives taking the needs and wishes of another into consideration. (We should be wary of cheap intimacy, formed instantly; that which comes without effort is lost just as easily.)

Although we cannot make an intimate relationship happen, we can always be open to the possibility; in fact, simply being open is what is needed. In the act of watching television, we can be open to the others watching with us or we can be in our own private space viewing the screen as if others were not present. Contrast a father and his sons watching a football game on television—rooting, cheering, dissecting plays—to a row of men in a bar all facing the screen without exchanging a word (except with the bartender, to order another). The former have an openness to each other. They are together in their watching, and thus, an intimacy is achieved. The men at the bar, on the other hand, have no risk of openness; their togetherness is limited to being in the same area.

Throughout this discussion, it should be obvious that in all intimacies, we have to be ourselves. In fact, being ourselves is *the* essential ingredient for intimacy. A test of whether intimacy is present or not is how a relationship makes us feel about ourselves. Do we like the self that we are when we are with a particular person? If the answer is yes, then we are on the road to intimacy.

I am often struck by themes of intimacy in religious traditions, both western and eastern, aboriginal and refined. A striking example is taken from the scriptural description in Isaiah 25:8, of God's relationship to humans, which reads "God will wipe away your tears." To wipe away a tear from someone is an exquisitely intimate act; it is not something you would do to a stranger. A mother would do it for her child, a lover for his beloved. If we believe God is omnipotent, then why not wipe away what is making us cry or, better, make it so that we never have to cry? But no, the phrase is "God will wipe away your tears." This does not imply a relationship of protection, defense, or of God running divine intervention, but rather, one of intimacy.

Whether taken literally or symbolically, intimacy with God speaks to the centrality of the need for intimacy. Some, hermit-like individuals, may make the pursuit of intimacy with God the central focus of their life; the rest of us recognize the need for other people and, although we may pursue God, see that intimacy with other people is not only essential for our well-being, but necessary for spirituality.

Too many of us think of intimacy within marriage as the ideal, with its socioreligious sanction for sexual intimacy presumably making it a "complete" relationship. Yet as we have seen previously in this chapter, no one person can satisfy all of our intimate needs, not even a spouse. As long as we think of marriage as the model for intimacy, the sexual aspect holds the focus. It seems to me, however, that friendship is a much better model for intimacy; we love the other without owning or possessing them.

Friendship does not demand exclusivity, as marriage usually does. It may be necessary for marriage in order to guarantee paternity and protect maternal interests, but exclusivity is destructive to friendship. When we seek or demand it in friendship, it arises from a fear of losing what we derive from that relationship, rather than out of love for the other. In our early teen years we form "best-friend" pacts, full of secrecy, excluding others from our special relationship. Mature love tends toward inclusiveness rather than exclusiveness: We want to connect other significant people in our lives to this special person. The love that any of us has to give is not a fixed quantity, diminished every time we love; rather, love is increased in the giving. The more we love, the more love we have to give; the more intimates we have, the more our capacity for intimacy expands.

Friendship does not necessarily involve a lifelong commitment. In our culture, marriage holds that quality, providing the stability needed to raise children. Yet commitment in friendship is essential, although it is generally open-ended, rather than lifelong. Some friendships end because of a change in interests of one or the other; others fall to geographic separations, or a misunderstanding. And then there are friendships that last a lifetime, despite obstacles and hindrances. Knowledge that a friendship may one day end ought never keep us from risking intimacy, however. Avoidance brought on by the fear of possible loss can be far more painful than any actual loss.

Blocks to Intimacy

We long for intimacy, search for it, hope for it, yet so often miss the opportunities. Why? Or, if we see the opportunities, why do we fail to respond? Or, if we respond, why do our attempts at intimacy end with failure? These important questions are not easily answered.

The historical images and folk tales that we were raised on offered rugged individualism and self-reliance as models for behavior, rather than interdependence and intimacy. Look at that authentic American folk hero, the cowboy (or the similarly revered Canadian Mountie): He is always alone, separated from his true love, totally self-reliant, needing no one, able to overcome any obstacle. If he is affectionate, it is with his horse or dog. Where are the values of love, intimacy, and dependable caring in this model? If we read the myth right, these values are peripheral to the really important things in life. This same myth defines women as on the fringe of the real action of life, patiently awaiting their man, often strong in character but subject to the weaknesses of males.

Add to this that the most difficult beliefs or behaviors to alter in each of us are those that are implicitly taught at home. Prejudices that are explicitly taught at home—like all blacks are lazy, or all Catholics are untrustworthy, or all Jews are mercenary—frequently get rejected by children when they confront the reality outside the home. But implicit behaviors, beliefs, and attitudes, like those around sexuality and intimacy, are more difficult to affect because the teaching is unconscious and taken for granted.

The truth is, however, that many of us had poor models of intimacy in our parents, grandparents, siblings, and extended families. This affects, usually unconsciously, how we relate as adults. The degree to which we respect and value others, how safe we feel in intimacy, our sexual expression—all of this is psychologically inhaled from what we learned within our family. Small wonder that much of becoming intimate as adults involves both unlearning negative behaviors and opening ourselves to relational reexperiencing.

Given that neither our culture nor our families may have prepared us well for adult intimacies, there are some common psychological blocks to forming and sustaining intimate relationships. I would like to discuss six of these.

Sexuality. The first block to intimacy is the fear of our sexuality. As we enter into a close relationship with another, our sexual feelings, or lack thereof, can be an issue. If sexual feelings make you uncomfortable, be they toward the same or opposite sex, then you are going to be constantly on guard, unable to be spontaneous in an encounter because of the need to inhibit your own sexual responsiveness. Of course, we all need to regulate our sexual expressiveness; but being relaxed about sexuality, having a feeling of security in our maleness or femaleness, means knowing that we are adequate as woman or man with no need to prove or demonstrate it. Also, sexual expression helps to convey our feelings for the other; we should not use it to capture or hold onto the other, whether within a marriage or a friendship.

If you ask any group of people where they learned about sex, only a few would reply "At home." Most would say they learned about sex on the street, from friends, or at school or church. But this is not true. Our first lessons on sex and sexuality are learned at home. We may learn how to "do it" outside of our home, but the basic lessons come from our families. For example, when your father came home from work and gave your mother a pat on the fanny, and she turned and gave him a big smile, that taught you more about sexuality than anything you learned from your friends. Even if sex itself was never mentioned in your family, that in itself was a potent lesson. Home is where our most basic, intuitive learning takes place.

Too many of us still struggle with the unconscious feeling that sex is "dirty" and "not nice." Although we consciously acknowledge the naturalness and appropriateness of sexual feelings and activity, there is a puritanical strain deep in the American psyche that looks on sexuality with distaste, if not downright disgust. Witness the sensitivity that both political and religious figures have for sexual revelations. We seem more sensitive to infidelities in our leaders than we are to abuses of power or unscrupulous affluence. Witness that, in spite of the sexual revolution and our increased sophistication, we still have difficulty imagining our parents as sexual. Even in the face of evidence, we would rather desexualize them to support an image of their being above "that kind of stuff."

That all of us have both a homosexual and a heterosexual drive within us (that is not to say that all of us are homogenital or heterogenital) is a generally accepted psychological tenet. We each may express these drives in different ways; but that there is some heterosexuality in the homosexual and some homosexuality in the heterosexual seems undeniable. If this is something we are not comfortable with, it can affect how we relate to one another, and can be a block to the formation of intimate relationships.

Anger. A second possible block to intimacy, although one that many people are better at coping with these days, is anger. Anger becomes problematic in two ways: the impulsive-explosive expression or the repressed-avoidant lack of expression. When anger is poorly controlled and impulsively explosive, others avoid us since we are not pleasant to be around. If we avoid any expression of anger, then we are going to avoid others because any close relating to another entails occasional stimulation of anger.

An example of this can be seen with parent/child relationships. To children, parents are gods, with the power of life and death, which makes any expression of anger threatening. Illustrative of this is the expression used by children around the world, "My parents will kill me if they find out." The child realizes that parents will not actually execute them, but symbolically, at least, parents still retain the power of life and death over their children. (Although, it should be noted that actual cases of parents murdering their child are not rare; even less rare are various forms of physical abuse viciously inflicted on children by parental figures.) For this reason, parental anger can be terrorizing and children may never get over this terror, even as adults.

A nurse came to consult with me about her inability to

construct a life for herself. She was in her late 30s, successful professionally, but living at home caring for aging parents. Her sense of gratitude toward her parents was genuine, as was her concern for their well-being. Strangely, though, she was unable to carry on a conversation with either of them.

She cooked, cleaned, provided them with niceties to enhance their enjoyment of life—but she could not talk to them beyond pleasantries about the weather and the latest news of one of their mutual friends. This did not happen with her friends and associates at work; she was known as a loquacious, outgoing person. But at home, she was quiet and non-communicative.

Through therapy, the nurse discovered that she was full of rage toward her parents, a leftover from the emotional abuse she received from them in her childhood. She loved her parents, of course; but we can be hurt deepest by those we love most. When the hurt is great, the anger is great and frequently crosses the boundary from anger to rage. Anger is the growl, a warning to the other to cease, a protective maneuver. Rage is always murderous; it is a roar that seeks to destroy the offender in language designed to commit the murder, albeit symbolically.

But how can you murder someone you love, even in words, and how do you reconcile murderous feelings with loving ones? The nurse solved the conflict by inhibiting her speech. If she did not control her speech, she feared the rage would come out and hurt her beloved parents. She was not consciously aware of her rage, or its conflict; she was aware only of her love and her silence.

Fear of expressing anger comes from three sources. Perhaps we are afraid of our anger, its intensity, and its destructive potential. If we permit even a little expression of it, we fear it will all pour out, like the boy who could not remove his finger from the dike lest he flood his village.

Or we fear that the anger of another will destroy us, like the child who thinks her parents "will kill her" if she makes them angry. As children, we shape our behavior into acceptable paths by learning what angered our parents and scrupulously avoiding it. Adolescents learn that they can risk parental anger, and not be "killed" by it. Although this creates difficulties for parents, it is essential learning for the adolescent so that as an adult, he or she can handle anger more appropriately. Through this process of trial and error, we find that we can handle the anger of others without destroying either ourselves or the relationships we value.

A third source of anger inhibition is a weak sense of self-worth; we need everyone to like us in order to feel likeable. If someone does not, then we see that as proof of our own defect and resulting unlikeableness. Since angry people are "not likeable," we can never show anger; we always have to "be nice."

Anger is not an easy emotion to deal with, but deal with it we must if we are to have close relationships. Although there is no "how to" applicable to all situations, some general principles can be helpful. First of all, we must be aware of when we are angry. For those who are accustomed to repressing anger, it is a major task to simply know and admit to themselves that they are angry. Next, we must make a decision about what we are going to do about our anger. Sometimes, it may be inappropriate or unwise to express it directly to the person who is making us angry, for a variety of reasons. However, if we choose to inhibit expression, it can be very helpful to have ways to remove the stress: someone to discuss our anger with, or some vigorous activity designed to expel the stress. It may be better to express anger directly, but it is unrealistic to think that this is always possible.

Most of us find it important to talk to the person who made us angry. A few simple rules can make this easier. The anger should be expressed in ways that respect the dignity of the other. This entails talking about our anger rather than about the other person's reprehensible behavior, and then letting the other respond, listening to what he or she says about their behavior. Often, a simple understanding of what motivated the other can dissipate the anger.

Next, avoid a win/lose situation; if both parties can walk away feeling that they have not lost (you do not need to win to feel you have not lost), the issues that evoked anger are more easily resolved. Finally, try to bring some closure to the issue. When closure is not achieved, the issue will tend to be replayed in your fantasy, re-evoking the feelings you hoped to resolve. Closure may be forgiveness, an expression of understanding, or even mutual agreement to avoid each other in the future; but some kind of bottom line should be reached.

Anger management is another one of those implicit learnings that occur in the family. Examining how your family dealt with anger and its expression can help you understand your conflict about it. We will further discuss the management of anger in another chapter, but for now, we need to understand that if we do not cope with anger appropriately it interferes with our ability to have intimate relationships.

Dependency. A third block to intimate relationships is the fear of dependency. Part of the process of maturation is our growth from a state of total dependence on others to one where we are self-reliant and self-responsible. This is not an easy process, and achieving it can be a hard-won victory we do not wish to relinquish. If we permit intimacy to happen, however, it creates a need for the other; we feel as if we cannot get along without the other, although we know that we can. And indeed, to lose intimacy with another once it has been established is a source of great pain. Psychoanalyst Erich Fromm speaks of this as a love not based on need, but need arising from love.

Much of marriage, especially in its early years, can be a struggle for domination, power, and control arising from a fear of becoming dependent on the other and losing our identity. Sexual promiscuity is also a defense against dependence, possibly arising from early life experiences where dependence became hurtful. Our culturally determined concept of masculinity contains elements of fiercely held independence—witness the cowboy myth—making men more prone to a stance of detachment, a refusal to surrender into the need for one another that intimacy both leads to and requires. Within the experience of intimacy, however, we discover that, although identity changes, individuality can deepen within the additional identities of spouse, lover, and friend.

Inadequacy. Another source of difficulty with intimacy, and the fourth block, is in having intense feelings of personal inadequacy that make us hide our true selves and wear masks in our interpersonal contacts. We have already alluded to this when we discussed the necessity of permitting oneself to be known within an intimate relationship. If we are burdened with self-hatred or feelings of inadequacy, we will either have difficulty risking true self-expression, or not trust the loving response that another gives. (Some call the latter "the Groucho Marx complex." When asked about his fraternal lodge affiliations, Groucho is reported to have said that he would never stoop so low as to join a club who was desperate enough to accept someone like him as a member.)

The area in which psychotherapy seems to be most helpful is in improving our self-image or self-esteem. This is the reason many therapy clients form intimate relationships for the first time in their lives toward the later stages of therapy. If the shame and self-hatred gets resolved, one can open up to intimacies.

Vulnerability. Closely allied to a defective sense of self is the need to be strong, a fear of being weak or vulnerable. This is the fifth block. Few of us would choose to be vulnerable; it is safer to be strong. I believe people play the lottery not so much for the 10 million dollar prize, but because they think that if they won the money they could tell everyone to "go to hell!" The winner would be invulnerable because of the security that lots of money appears to offer.

We are not, however, invulnerably strong. As creatures, we are terrifyingly vulnerable; nature has not provided us with many defenses, other than our brains (which make us aware of how really vulnerable we are!). Wars, random violence, oppressive poverty, rejection, abandonment, weather, pollution, death— the list of "predators" is endless. Every time we get in our cars and drive to work, school, or shopping we are prey to unforeseeable events. We take reasonable measures to protect ourselves and others, but there is no way to be totally invulnerable.

Being intimate involves an act of surrender, the ultimate expression of vulnerability. The risk of rejection, loss, humiliation, and powerlessness is always present. If our fear of weakness is so great that it makes us hold onto the illusion of invulnerability, then we can never have truly intimate relationships.

Narcissism. Lastly, let me describe the sixth block, a psychiatric malady that invariably inhibits the formation of intimate relationships. This is narcissism or, more correctly, narcissistic personality disorder. Although it draws its name from the mythological tale of Narcissus (and understanding the myth can help in understanding the malady), it should not be confused with a self-love, nor a falling in love with oneself. Narcissism has very little to do with love of self or others, except in so far as it renders someone incapable of having sufficient empathy to be able to love another.

Narcissistic personality disorder is a *bona fide* psychological condition, often difficult to diagnosis accurately because its traits are, to some degree, found in all of us. The principal feature of the narcissistic personality is an exaggerated sense of one's own self-worth, resulting in an unrealistic belief in that person's specialness and entitlement. Other people exist only to meet the needs of the narcissist. If ignored or not properly acknowledged as special, narcissists become readily upset and demanding. They are apt to place blame for their lack of achievement on factors outside themselves, and are often enraged over even minor negative criticism.

Many personality theorists believe that narcissism is a reaction formation, a way to cover up intense feelings of personal inferiority and a fear that the self is really nothing. Narcissists construct a self of exaggerated significance as a bulwark against the possibility that their fears of "nothingness" may be true. This creates an excessive need for affirming admiration in order to convince themselves that they have value and are not worthless.

Because it defends against an ever-present fear, the need for approval becomes insatiable, and much of the narcissist's energy is committed to gaining praise from others. He or she seeks out friendships only with those who feed their egos with flattering evaluations. Since the narcissist is preoccupied with his or her own need for recognition, the ability to empathetically relate to another is seriously impaired.

All of us have some degree of self-doubt, along with fears

of inadequacy and the suspicion that we may be incompetent. This is why we have a sense of elation when we are praised and recognized by others, and why we feel wounded when we are ignored or negatively judged. Each of us battles against the fear of nothingness, and seeks outside confirmation that we really are somebody, that we have significance.

Secondary narcissism, although a more mature condition, still inhibits spiritual growth. This is where narcissism moves from "me" needing recognition as superior and uniquely special, to having what is "mine" so recognized. Be it our family, our country, our religion, our friends, our race, or our possessions; this recognition overcomes a fear of personal worthlessness. Witness the intense emotional reaction some people have to the burning of the flag, an act defended by the Supreme Court as consitutionally protected dissent. Their reaction is often not because flag-burning is an insult to "my *country*," but rather, an insult to "*my* country," an assault to self-esteem.

Secondary narcissism is often rationalized as pride, be it civic or otherwise, and some of this is fine. We can be proud of our church, country, ethnic group, or the like for its courage, for what it achieves, or for the stands it takes. These groups and organizations, however, do not define us. Belonging to a group may say something about us, or about aspects of us, but we do not derive our self-esteem from membership in a particular group. When labels are the source of our significance, we have secondary narcissism.

Narcissism is a treatable, albeit serious and difficult, psychiatric disorder. There may be slight traces of it in all of us, but the disorder is not present in everyone. I mention it here as an obvious hindrance to forming intimacies, but it is not in the same category as the other blocks to intimacy. Narcissism is a definite disorder, where the others are not. Rather, they are part of the human condition, and although psychotherapeutic intervention can help, it is not required. There is a great space for self-help with the first five. I do not believe this is true for narcissism.

Questions for Discussion

1. List the first names of three people whom you would label as your intimates. What is there about them that permits intimacy to happen? Could, or would, you seek others with the same qualities?

2. List 10 words you associate with "loneliness." Put the list aside for a day, then examine it with someone else, if possible. What does this list tell you about the sources of loneliness in your life? What can others see in that list that might help you better understand your loneliness?

3. In what way are you a friend to others? Are you as good a friend to others as you would expect them to be to you? What do you expect from a "good friend"?

4. It is said that the greatest barrier to intimacy is our fear of it. What blocks to intimacy can you identify within yourself? What lessons about intimacy did you learn within the family you grew up in? What steps can you take so that these do not control you? How can you help the persons you love overcome their blocks to intimacy?

Chapter 3

Stress

Stress is a major health problem in North America, indicted in almost every illness or disease that afflicts us, from heart disease to the flu. If we are under sustained stress, the immune system is weakened, making us more susceptible to bacteria and viruses. Stress also contributes to the wear and tear of organ systems, straining already vulnerable bodies to the breaking point, rendering them less resistant to trauma.

Indirectly, stress increases health hazards by encouraging use of substances like nicotine, alcohol, psychotropic medications, and illicit street drugs. Stress is connected to anxiety, burnout, depression, and can be a precipitant to acute psychiatric distress. It reduces our efficiency at work, and causes family strife as it infects relationships with increased irritability, distractions, and general unhappiness.

The smaller stresses that we routinely meet can accumulate into a deadly combination that can break us. An event that makes us "lose it" is likely only the last event in a long chain of stresses, the proverbial straw that breaks the camel's back. A popular test for stress lists occurrences ranging from a lack of hot water for our morning shower, to job loss, divorce, or the death of a loved one, giving a numerical value to each; if our score shows that we have too many stressful situations in our lives, we may be in serious danger.

When I am asked to speak by a particular group, stress is the topic most frequently requested. I have discussed this topic with school teachers and administrators, whose level of stress is understandably high; but also with cloistered nuns living in community, one of the least likely groups we expect to suffer from stress. Yet this should not surprise us, however, since the cause of stress is related more to the perception of a situation than to the situation itself. A surgeon may feel stressed by the responsibility he carries in the operating room, while a nun may feel stress because of the way the nun next to her in chapel rattles her beads.

From the description above, it may seem like the most desirable thing to do is to get rid of stress entirely. No way; we could not tolerate it. Look at how much effort we expend in creating stress for ourselves. We love movies that frighten us, books that hold us in suspense, gambling, a mountain climb, all kinds of daredevilry, competitive activities, risk taking, and challenges. If we avoid all stress, we become bored (which itself is a stress), and seek relief through something stimulating (a stress). Not only is stress unavoidable, it is undesirable to avoid it. The only truly stressless time of our life will be when six of our friends pick us up by the handles of our coffin and carry us down the aisle.

Physiologically, stress gives us a degree of pleasant stimulation that, in some personalities, has the potential to become addictive. When we are under stress, two endorphins—epinephrine and norpinephrine—are released in the brain. These create a state of pleasurable euphoria similar to what one feels when sexually aroused. The same endorphins are released when we are in danger, whether physical or psychological. Since the physical reaction to these endorphins is identical, whether the stress is "good" or "bad" depends on how it is interpreted by the one experiencing it. The effect of these endorphins may be part of the physiological mechanisms that make us seek thrills and avoid boredom.

There is an optimal level of stress that each of us functions best at, and we struggle to maintain that level. When stress increases beyond our optimum we increase our effort to bring the level down. The effort we expend to increase, maintain, or reduce stress becomes the source of significant advancements in science and industry. Subsequently, stress fuels the advancement of knowledge by becoming a motivator of effort.

Stress itself is not a problem, even though it has the potential to harm us. What we need are effective ways to cope with stress.

Let me create a scene for you that illustrates how our stress impulses work on a very primitive level. Imagine one of our aboriginal ancestors, a "cave man," if you will. He gets up in the morning and comes out of his cave, leaving his mate and child behind, still sleeping. It is a beautiful day; the air is clean and the sun is shining. He walks to a stream that runs about 80 feet from the cave, takes a drink of sweet, cool water, splashes some on his face, and is filled with a sense of peace and security. He walks back toward the cave when suddenly he sees a saber-toothed tiger standing between him and the mouth of the cave, eyeing him with a hungry look.

What happens next to this man? Immediately, his autonomic nervous system reacts to bring on the so-called "flight or fight" response. Adrenaline is dumped into his blood stream, bringing about a host of physical reactions: His pupils contract to sharpen vision; lung capacity expands to take in more oxygen; His heart beats more rapidly, pumping oxygen around his body faster; pores open and pour cooling sweat onto his skin; his bowel and bladder may evacuate themselves; his muscles tense. This series of physical changes insures that if he chooses flight he will run faster and further before exhaustion; if he chooses fight, he will fight with greater strength and endurance. This is all part of the body's defense system designed to support our survival.

Nature intends "flight" as the primary option, because running away gives us a better chance at survival. Notice any animal that is startled with a potential danger: It will invariably opt to run, unless there is an overriding reason not to. The man in our story, though, cannot run; his mate and child are in the cave, and he must protect them. "Fight" is his only choice.

As his body tenses for the encounter, he moves toward the tiger, crouched and preparing for the kill. At that moment, the man spies a wedge-shaped rock in the sand. He reaches for it as the tiger starts its leap, and smashes the rock into the tiger's head just before its teeth are at his throat. The tiger crashes to the ground, dead.

A sense of elation and relief floods the man's body, as homeostasis returns; adrenaline ceases its course through his body and the flight/fight reactions all return to normal. After he stops to catch his breath, he is quickly back to the sense of peace and well-being he had at the stream, with an added sense of elation because now he has tiger meat, as well.

Now, let us take a look at modern man. He gets up in the

morning, and looks out the window at the yellowish haze hanging over the neighborhood because of the recent atmospheric inversion. There's not much in the refrigerator to eat since he was working too late yesterday to stop at the supermarket, and the water from the tap has a funny taste to it—probably the chlorine they decided to add at the last city council meeting. As he is thinking about the heavy day he has in front of him, still unsure how to cope with the issues left over from yesterday, the phone rings. It is his boss, who says, in a stridently angry voice, "I want to see you in my office in 20 minutes!"

There is his saber-toothed tiger, and his body has the same reaction, the flight/fight response. Flight rushes through his mind—How fast can I get money out of the bank and catch a flight to southern California?—but he has obligations, family to support, responsibilities. He cannot flee. But, it is important to remember that this is always nature's first option, therefore, we always think of it.

He rushes to the office, and stands in front of the boss's desk: There the attack begins. "I am so sick of the way you do your work here," shouts the boss. "My 12-year-old could have prepared a better report than the one you submitted. Didn't they teach you how to write English at the rinky-dink university you went to?" The harangue continues. Unable to get in a word of explanation, the man looks down onto the desk, and there, in arm's reach, is a wedge-shaped lead paperweight...

But, what is he to do? The law does not look kindly on murder; besides, he needs this job. He cannot risk offending the boss, and so he does not rage back, or even let his anger show: He stands there and takes it. Herein lies the problem. There is no release for his bodily reaction to this stress. Not that he should use the paperweight, hop a flight to California, or tell the boss to take his job and stick it; but now he may well leave the boss's office and, for hours, days, weeks, months, or even years, continue reliving the event in fantasy, replaying all kinds of scenes about what he would like to have said or done. And because it was not expelled, the state of readiness for flight or fight remains.

This chronic state of arousal weakens our immunity and wears down organ systems, a physical and psychological effect that is a contributing factor to every disease known to us. Living in today's civilization imposes extensive and severe restrictions on our more natural, impulse-motivated reactions. Stress is not the culprit; civilization is.

Dealing with Stress

Since it is impossible, and not very desirable, to return to the state of primitive humanity, we must find ways to cope with stress that are more in keeping with the norms and laws of our present-day world. Each of us has our saber-toothed tigers, be they within our work or profession, family, government, or relationship. How we choose to fight—or take flight from—those tigers is our task in coping with stress.

We need to identify our stresses, recognizing that how we perceive and explain them are larger contributing factors to distress than the events themselves. As we look at our stresses and make some choices—perhaps major life choices focused on living with less stress—we must evaluate how much stress is arising out of an attempt to sustain a self-image that may be neither sustainable nor desirable. Who are we trying to impress, and why? Our need for achievement, recognition, affirmation, and appearing better than others can generate more stress than a task or its surrounding circumstances. Identifying these types of stressors may require more of an inner search than an external one.

Unpredictable events are a much greater source of stress than predictable ones, probably because of a need we have to feel in control. Since so much of life is unpredictable, we can go for long periods of time with our stress levels on overdrive. What to do? For most of us, getting our level of stress down to normal makes a lot more sense than trying to avoid excessive stress.

Alcohol is a popular de-stressor. Since it is chemically an anaesthetic, it numbs us to the distress. At least part of the health benefit of moderate alcohol usage is likely in its capacity to bring down our levels of stress. Problems can occur, however, because of alcohol's tolerance-building feature; the more you use, the more you need to drink to achieve the same result. The same is true of any other chemical method of stress reduction: fine in the short term, but full of potential hazards if relied on for long periods.

A president of France was once asked, "If you had one piece of advice to give to a world leader, what would it be?" Without hesitation, he answered, "To listen to Mozart for a half-hour each day!" Music is a potent de-stressor, wrapping us in a cocoon, allowing our feelings to soar wherever the music takes us, free of the rational syllogisms that dominate so much of our life. A piece of music becomes "classic" precisely because of its capacity to move us beyond the bounds of our stress-filled lives into moments where nothing matters but the feelings that flood our consciousness. For a time we are caught up in the music; we are beyond stress.

Many other activities help alleviate stress. Meditation, especially centering or inner-focusing meditation, can be very effective in bringing stress to a manageable level. Prayer helps us to cope with stress, beyond any other positive result it might produce. Techniques of muscle relaxation and deep breathing can be of significant help, since it is impossible for one's body to feel relaxed and tense at the same time. Regular long walks in peaceful settings, looking at great art, and recreational sports, such as golf, tennis, racquetball, or jogging, can counter stresses that arise from work. Exercise programs function well not only to discharge energy that stress permits to accumulate, but to psychologically provide an escape from the self-absorption contained in all stresses.

The Need for Self-Expression

Permit me to describe how debilitating and pernicious stress can be, especially where it lacks a clearly identifiable stressor. Some time ago I received a phone call from a woman requesting an appointment. Her voice betrayed a kind of urgency, so I rearranged my schedule to see her at the earliest possible date. She arrived 15 minutes early for the appointment and when I went out to the waiting area she was sitting primly, browsing through a magazine.

The woman was in her early forties, attractively dressed in a business suit, with well-maintained hair and makeup sensibly applied. She did not seem especially depressed or overly anxious, but had a sober, no-nonsense demeanor. The only other remarkable thing about her was her eyes; they were surrounded by worry lines, the eyes of an older person, filled with resigned surrender. After introducing myself to her and shaking her hand, we walked into my office.

When we were seated, the woman relayed that she was a fourth-grade teacher, and had come to see me because her principal, who also happened to be a friend, strongly suggested that she may need to address certain issues in her life. The women then described those things that were of concern. She was becoming increasingly irritated at her students, on occasion losing her temper with them or their parents. She felt frazzled by the amount of work piling up on her, and by the loss of her teacher's aide due to budget restraints. With her colleagues, her usual playful humor had given way to a more caustic wit, and she avoided the staff room whenever possible.

Physically, this woman's sleep was restless, and she had gained twelve pounds in the last five months. Further, she was becoming increasingly disinterested in any sort of social life. The results of a recent physical exam were non-remarkable, lacking suggestion of any early menopausal changes. Except for moderately elevated blood pressure, she was in excellent physical health.

She talked about her husband, a successful, 47-year-old lawyer, who was a good provider and father to their two children, ages 13 and 10. He took the marriage seriously, and although a bit over-involved in his work, tried to be present to her and the children, acknowledging the full-time nature of his wife's work and sharing the household responsibilities. She felt that at times he did not live up to her expectations—in his efforts to be a good husband and father he was a bit compulsive and mechanical, doing all the right things, but often without the emotional warmth and support she needed. Yet she realized that compared to many other people she had it made. Then why was she so unhappy?

As she talked about her life, the day-to-day routines, her short- and long-term goals, her realities and her fantasies, it did not take long for a picture to emerge. This was an intelligent, passionate woman, with a *joie de vivre* squelched in a life of routines, schedules, and imposed demands. This woman, like most, was a complex blend of the wild, uninhibited seductress, the responsible, caring wife and mother, and the serious, commited professional. Stress was destroying her, but this stress arose from her infidelity to herself. Life had no significant enjoyment for her because it lacked self-expression; everything was done for some externally imposed purpose.

None of us can avoid routines, demands, and schedules; but these should serve us, not we them. As human beings, we need to find some space in our lives where we can break out of schedules, cut loose, and take back ownership of our lives. This woman did not need to end her marriage, find a new career, or go to the South Pacific to find herself. If she did any of these, she would have found herself in the same unhappy state she was then in. What she needed to do was to start living it responsibly. Rather than permitting the perceived expectations of others to control her, she needed to rediscover herself and bring that person to her work, her home, and her social life.

Although it was not until much later that I met her husband, behind his highly scheduled, achievement-orientated, living-up-to-expectations life was a passionate, carefree, and spontaneously enthusiastic man who was also squelching his own character. Both he and his wife were successful as professional people; where they were failing was as human beings. They both needed to rediscover that something soulful which drew them together and still held them together. Both alone and with each other, they had to build a more balanced life.

Part of this process is to cultivate a rich personal life, full of what we find enriching. Whether it be musical concerts, plays, travel, theater, sports, literature, movies, novels, mountain climbing, walking beaches, restaurants, poker games, or being with children—each of us must find what we can be passionate about, and actively incorporate these things into our lives.

The overstressed condition called "burnout" happens frequently with people whose work requires them to place the welfare of others ahead of their own wishes and desires. It is found in professions wherein you are continuously giving, often without getting much back. Burnout happens to nurses, physicians, psychotherapists, teachers, social workers, clergy, and, yes, parents too. We see it in policemen, public servants, secretaries, waiters, and prison guards. All of us need sources of nourishment wherein we are replenished, else we will have nothing to give and, likely, end up harming the very people we are supposed to be helping.

Friends can be a major source of nourishment and should play an important role in the life of a caregiver. Often, when those in the helping professions do not enrich their lives with friends, they turn toward those with whom they have a professional relationship to meet their personal needs. Therapists turn to clients, teachers to students, or clergy to parishioners, and find themselves in ethically questionable relationships which are fraught with danger. These kinds of liaisons usually end up being unsatisfying at best; at worst, they become harmful to one or the other party.

One prominent facet of the healthiest people I know is that they never let their job, or profession, define who they are. What they do for a living makes up only a part of who they are: They are life-involved people, not job-involved ones. They give equal concern to their personal life, family life, and professional life; they are intent on living their lives according to their own agenda, not one imposed from outside.

I will repeat my conviction that stress is not the problem; the problem is that we do not cope with stress as well as we could. We live lives that do not provide the experiences and spaces that enable us to not only tolerate, but even to thrive on the pressures and challenges that confront us. Stress is like saturated fat or chocolate in our diet; we crave it, but we can get sick on it if we do not balance it with other life-enhancing experiences.

If the primary essential for wellness is taking self-responsibility for ourselves, nowhere else is that more clear than in coping with stress. Too many of us suffer from excessive levels of stress; too many of us complain about the stress we live under. But what are we doing about it? Escaping all stress is neither possible nor desirable. What is necessary is that we live our lives as our own, not as if they were orchestrated by someone or something else. We must take responsibility for who we are and how we are going to live our lives amid the demands, stresses, and routines of daily life.

Questions for Discussion

1. List, in their order of significance, five sources of stress in your life. What irrational statements, e.g., "I must be perfect," "Everyone must admire me," "It will be disastrous if ...," are you repeating to yourself that cause, or aggravate, each of those stresses? Is there a rational statement to replace each of the irrational ones?

2. How do you cope with the stresses of work? What do you need to do to ensure that de-stressing moments or activities have as much priority in your life as those activities or moments that raise your level of stress?

3. "Stress is not the culprit, civilization is." What does this statement mean to you? How does this affect your view of your own stress and help you find more balance in your lifestyle? Are you buying into social myths that you truly do not believe in? Are you living your life responsibly?

4. Anger is a major stressor. How do you express your angry feelings? Are you direct or indirect? How do you "let off steam" when circumstances make it impossible (or imprudent) to express the anger directly?

CHAPTER 4

EMOTIONS

It is with good reason that in our society we make "emotional illness" synonymous with "mental illness." For most who feel psychologically unwell, the problem is with their emotions or feelings, not with their thought or reasoning processes, or in their intuitive or sensate capacities. Feelings are difficult to cope with, and many of us get stuck in our attempts to deal with them. That is not to say that logical thinking, misinterpretations, or faulty cognitions cannot cause difficulty; however, the difficulty usually lies in what these make us feel, rather than in what they make us think.

Maladaptive behavioral reactions based on misinformation, misunderstanding, or nonrational thinking are relatively easy to deal with through correcting our information, addressing the faulty basis for our understanding, or rethinking our position. Much more difficult is dealing with our affect, our all-too-often messy feelings. These can become so difficult to cope with we actually disconnect from them, so that, although our body continues to register the feeling, our minds no longer permit us to be aware of them. We adapt to a chronic emotion in that it continues to affect our bodies, but we lose awareness of its presence; illustrative of this is a constant smell that we are no longer aware of until someone calls our attention to it.

Each of us has, or ought to have, the full array of human feelings: anger, sadness, joy, fear, enthusiasm, jealousy, rage, pity, envy, surprise, ecstasy, frustration, embarrassment. To quote the Roman playwright, Terence, "Nothing human is foreign to us." Some feelings are pleasant to have, like joy, affection, or infatuation; others are unpleasant, like anger, jealousy, sadness. Feelings come unbidden, intended by nature to make us do, or not do, some action. We may have a measure of choice regarding that action, but none around having, or not having, the feeling.

To some degree, the expression of feelings must be controlled and regulated: The hysteric, for example, is in need of greater emotional control. And, our expression of emotion is further regulated by social factors; for example, how we express our feelings at work is (usually) different from how we express those same feelings with a close friend. But, for the majority of people, overcontrolled emotions are more problematic than a lack of emotional control. Obsessional and compulsive disorders—symptoms of an overcontrolled emotional life—are significantly greater in the Western world than are impulse-control disorders. To not feel requires repressing our emotions, a mental mechanism whereby we force something out of consciousness. We may choose not to express a feeling, but unless it is discharged somehow, that feeling will stay with us.

One of the problems with repression is that we cannot be selective about it; repression is always inclusive of all our feelings. If we repress our anger, we also repress our joy; if jealousy, then also affection. We cannot refuse to experience the unpleasant feelings and keep only the pleasant ones. Our *joie de vivre*, our passion, comes from the full bouquet of emotions found in the human psyche. As former Israeli prime minister Golda Meir said, "He who cannot cry with his whole heart cannot laugh, either."

Too often we deny a feeling, disown it, and soon, subjectively, we cease to experience it. This action is usually directed toward the difficult and discomforting emotions, like anger, rage, and jealousy, or sadistic and masochistic inclinations. Having negative feelings may clash with our self-image, making us feel ignoble, petty, or "bad." We may also repress because fear of possible consequences makes a particular feeling "dangerous" to us. Feeling comes reflexively; the best I can do to stop it is to block my awareness and deny, to myself and others, that I have such an emotion. You may have had the experience of having to speak in front of a group of people, thinking you were calm and relaxed, but then realizing that your palms were sweaty, a sure sign of anxiety. You repressed the feeling of fear, but not the fear itself.

Our minds engage us in this type of denial to help us get through difficult situations. We may find ourselves in a threatening situation, but remain calm, focused, and rational throughout; it is only after the threat has passed that we let down emotionally. This is a valuable process, often facilitating our actual survival. Stories of men in battle are replete with incidents of calmness through crises, followed by intense and debilitating emotional collapse. But when emotional avoidance becomes a habitual, day-in and day-out process for us, this avoided affect builds up and is apt to sweep over us in one, big, vague feeling of *ennui*. All life then becomes a drag; we go through the days automatically, like robots.

Gradually, we become aware that we are depressed, and have been for so long that we do not remember what it feels like not to be. We are able to function—the depression is not yet of major proportion—but we find ourselves awake at 2:00 a.m., anxious and wondering if this is all life has to offer, overwhelmed by work, home, family, and friends, but too frightened to make a change. We may fantasize about some avenue of escape, or that some chance event (like winning the lottery) will rescue us from all this. But it never happens, and we continue to live in "quiet desperation."

This kind of depression often comes when we are not living out our own drama, allowing ourselves to be merely players in someone else's story. We live our lives according to another's agenda, twisting ourselves in Procrustean fashion to fit in. We may even have heeded the exhortations of the Delphic oracle to "know thyself," but have not taken the next step and permitted this self to be. These relatively mild, but chronic, depressions rob us of the peace and satisfaction that life can bring. Peripheral cures, like moving to a new area, finding a new job, divorcing, or having an affair, may bring temporary respite, but soon we find ourselves right back in the same dead-end state of immobilizing *ennui*.

An Unexplained Depression

The president of a major corporation once asked me to see if I could help one of his vice-presidents. The vice-president, "one of the nicest guys you'd ever want to meet," had recently been hospitalized with a major depression at age 56, from which he was not recovering. There was no prior family history of depression, and no discernable external event that could account for his present level of despair. A physical examination turned up no negative results. He had been given several trials of different antidepressants, as well as a series of electroconvulsive therapy; all resulted in no significant improvement.

I first met this man in his hospital room. He was seated at a small writing desk, staring downward, and he barely acknowledged my presence. He looked somewhat older than his years, with gray uncombed hair, dressed in baggy pants and an oversized jersey which looked like they had not been changed in weeks. I introduced myself and inquired about his feelings; he looked toward the ceiling, shook his head, and told me that he did not understand what was happening to him. Appearing to be on the verge of tears, he was sincerely frightened by his confusion and helplessness. Conversation was difficult, as he could not speak of anything beyond his despair and lack of understanding about his sudden low mood.

After this initial meeting, we met daily for 10 to 15 minutes, gradually increasing our time together as the man was more able to sustain contact with me. When he was finally released from the hospital, we continued therapy on a twice-weekly basis. Here the story of his life began to unfold.

The man had grown up on a farm in the midwest, among a family of hardworking, dedicated people whose entire life centered on farming. These decent people lived by strict "oughts" and "shoulds," and there was no abuse, neglect, or even unkindness in his early life. What was striking, though, was that his family seemed more like two-dimensional characters in a Grant Wood painting, than flesh-and-blood human beings.

The man had started working for the company right out of college, and gave himself totally to his job; he was an ideal "company man." Personally, he was a pleasant man, non-abrasive and affirming of others; people enjoyed his companionship, although he rarely socialized. He had never married, and lived with his 59-year-old brother, with whom he took regular vacations.

As the story of this man's life unfolded, it impressed me that his was an unremarkable, nontraumatic life story. Nothing untoward had ever happened to him; he had no complaints, was generally happy, and accepted whatever life brought his way. There was nothing he would do differently if he had to live his life over again. During all our conversations, he never had a rude word for anyone; he was kindness personified. Yet I soon began to realize that here was a unidimensional man: Where were his angers, his resentments, his jealousies? There was no passion in him at all; in fact, he showed no intense reaction to anything. I saw a hint of emotion only twice, and both times concerned the company he had given his life to.

Two years prior to my client's depression, a new president had been named to the company. My client, a vice-president with over 30 years invested in the company, was not even considered for the job. I asked him if he had had any feelings about this, and he replied, "Of course not! Why would I want that headache?" Note that even though I had asked him about his feelings, his response was actually a denial of any feeling. More emotion surfaced, however, when I probed more deeply. When I asked him, incredulously, "You weren't even considered for the presidency?" a tear came to his eye. But he quickly stifled it, shook his head, and pulled himself together: "I wouldn't even *want* the job!"

The second emotional crack came a few sessions later, while the man talked about the company and his concerns about its economic future. I made a remark which caught him off-guard: "Boy, you really give everything you have to that company, don't you?" His head snapped up to look me in the eye, and he said, "You'd better believe it!" The feeling contained in his statement was remarkable for him, a mixture of anger, frustration, and disappointment. He did not go any further with this reaction, but his emotions had flashed, if only momentarily.

Over the months, the man's depression lifted, at first slowly, then all of a sudden. He decided to make some major life changes, which included retiring from the company and opening his own consulting firm. He stopped therapy when he "felt himself" again, in spite of my reservations. I still hear from him, a card and brief note at Christmas time. He has remained depression free, and sounds happier than when I knew him.

I wish I could give you some clever psychodynamic explanation as to what caused his depression and what made it cease, but I cannot. Maybe the medication finally had some effect; or perhaps a biochemical imbalance in his brain spontaneously righted itself; or maybe he was the one in three people who recover from depression no matter what treatment they receive. My hunch is that I companioned him through an experience of affect that he did not make me privy to.

During the course of his depression, this man, who was significantly divorced from his affect, retouched a part of it and on some level experienced that it was all right. In giving his life to the company, he lived according to an agenda that was not his own. This included self-submission to an external ideal that did not permit him to see the legitimacy of his own aspirations, or acknowledge his feelings when they were thwarted.

Through therapy he let himself touch some of his angers, resentments, feelings of being cheated, possibly even foolishness for giving away so much of himself. In that process, he was able to reclaim himself for himself. He will never become a person who wears his emotions on his sleeve, but he can now permit himself to feel without it assaulting his self-esteem. Therein his recovery lay.

Knowing what we are feeling, being able to admit it to ourselves without any self-loathing, is essential to our well-being. It is also critical to accept those pieces of ourselves that, likely, will never be expressed. The potential for all behavior is inside each of us; we all have what the Jungians call a "dark side," the inverse of the good face we present to the world. We must look at the parent who murders her or his child, the person who sexually exploits a child, or the serial killers who commit unimaginable acts and know that, under certain circumstances, we are capable of the same behavior.

The more aware we are of our darker side, the less likely it is to find release since, knowing our own potential for evil, we can take steps to guard against acting on these negative impulses. Many of us have had the experience of being hurt by someone—such as a teacher, relative, or politician—who saw themselves as saintly, above reproach, when in fact they were quite sadistic and abusive, and hid behind a facade of altruism. Those who deny their dark side or are unaware of it are often the perpetrators of the greatest evil.

Perhaps our capacity for evil expands apace with our capacity for good. The 20th century has taken great strides in addressing the welfare of our brothers and sisters, the powerless, and the vulnerable. We have made tremendous progress in providing for children and the elderly with child welfare laws, improved retirement plans, medical care for the disadvantaged, and public assistance for those with physical, psychological, or economic handicaps. This century has seen great gains in the humanization of life, perhaps more than any previous century.

On the other hand, our century has also seen evil in unprecedented proportions: the holocaust of the Jews, the eastern Europeans, and the Russian dissidents during World War II; the massacres over the last 30 years of southeast Asians; the recent carnage of the wars in Rwanda and Bosnia; and all those systematically put to death because of their race, ethnicity, political beliefs, or religious heritage.

These holocausts were perpetrated by people just like you and me, not by some monsters, aberrants from the evolutionary process. The potential is in each of us to have been a perpetrator in any of these crimes. But so, too, is the potential to be a caring, concerned, responsible brother or sister to all humans. None of us is exclusively saint or sinner; we are blends of both, hopefully striving for one over the other.

Questions for Discussion

1. What feelings do you find difficult to accept in yourself, or let others know about? What do these feelings make you feel about yourself? What kind of person would you be if you did not have these feelings? Is this really true?

2. Are you depressed? Maybe not a clinical depression; but is there a lack of joy in you, a feeling of boredom or "is that all there is?" Is the answer to why you feel this way in this chapter?

3. Take a quiet moment and focus on each of your senses, shutting everything out except that sense. Stay 3 to 5 minutes in each sense, gently asking yourself, "What are my eyes seeing?" "What are my ears hearing?" "What is my nose smelling?" "What is my mouth tasting?" "What is my skin feeling?" Later, take the exercise inside your body: "What feelings am I experiencing?" "What is my body saying to me?" Let this simple exercise help you lose your mind and discover your body.

4. There is an aphorism that says "What I hate most in others, are the things inside myself that I despise." What do your hates teach you about yourself? Can you find a greater tolerance for others in owning your own propensity to evil?

CHAPTER 5

SHAME

It is a harsh world we are forced to enter, and it immediately begins to shape us in ways that will facilitate our adaptation to it. Since sex is the major determinant of personality development, the answer to the question, "Is it a boy or a girl?" probably does more to affect our subsequent learning and behavioral patterns than anything else that happens to us.

Sigmund Freud's theories on human behavior saw sexual repression (plus an aggressive/destructive tendency) as being at the heart of all neurotic (and psychotic) life adaptations. He constructed an elaborate theory of how sexual energy seeking expression determines personality development out of his experience within his medical and psychiatric practice.

Freud's patients showed him the consequences of sexual repression as an attempt to resolve the conflict between their erotic fantasies and wishes, and sociocultural expectations.

We need to keep in mind, however, the culture of Freud's era. The latter part of the 19th and early 20th centuries were, at heart, Victorian, with much sexual repression required. Nice people, especially if you were female, did not have sexual wishes and erotic fantasies. Sex was a duty, filled with a minimum of enjoyment.

In a variety of denominations, sex was prohibited at certain seasons. Married clergy sinned if they had sex on the day prior to celebrating the Eucharist. Most sexual acts which today are seen as normative were tabooed, and elaborate precautions to protect "purity" were instituted, and quickly institutionalized. Some religions taught that permitting sexual enjoyment was an indulgence of human weakness, at least a venial sin, even when the partner is one's spouse.

Secular society, for its own purposes, readily supported the repressive sexual atmosphere. To have children, to create a family, was an obligation in an atmosphere that was asexual, or at least pretended to be. In some strata of society, even the legs on the piano had to be covered less they stimulate erotic thoughts in the innocent.

Freud's ultimate contribution to psychotherapy was in pointing out how important sexuality is to us, from birth through old age. Today we see additional significant issues for our development; given the climate of his time, however, it is understandable that Freud moved to the conclusion that repression of prohibited sexual desires lay at the heart of all neurosis.

Victorianism still lingers among us, but we are much more open, able to talk about sexuality, and acknowledge our wishes and desires, even when they conflict with behavioral expectations. People less and less see any nobility in attempting an asexual adjustment to life; we are more likely to challenge sexual avoidance as evading responsibility or avoiding intimacy.

As we made better sexual adaptations, however, we moved into a period when anger became the despised emotion. Especially in the early post-World War II years, perhaps in reaction to the horror and deprivation of that time, "being nice" became the prevailing dogma, and anger was seen as incompatible with niceness.

Overall in this period, "being liked" and "getting along" were the primary goals of many child-rearing practices. Schools were expected not only to educate and prepare for a vocation, they were also expected to do social engineering, teaching children to suppress (or better repress) not just anger, but other feelings as well. Tolerance, cooperation, having a pleasant personality, being polite, were all seen as part of the socialization goals of schools. In practice, they meant teaching children that anger is a bad emotion. The prevailing culture moved into a new Victorianism with "no anger" replacing "no sex" as the moral imperative.

Small wonder that psychodynamic theories and therapists began to focus on anger—without neglecting sexuality—and began encouraging a more liberating attitude toward this emotion too. "Get it out!" "Say what you feel!" became the encouraging cry. Anger, with its more potent cousin rage, was seen as the culprit, not only in psychological distress, but in physiological issues as well. It was seen as a factor, if not cause, in such diverse illnesses as heart attacks, strokes, cancer, arthritis, colitis, ulcers, high blood pressure, and migraine headaches. Depression was described as anger turned back onto the self; suicide was seen as murderous rage vented inward; anxiety was a fear of retaliation for unconscious hostile wishes, and so on.

As a culture, we are getting better in dealing with anger. Most recognize the inevitability of angry feelings, acknowledging the need to develop ways of socially acceptable expression. As a result, people are feeling less conflicted about coping with anger, and fewer problems of this nature are showing up in the mental health practitioner's office. Although we are a long way from dealing constructively with anger, we are better than we were a few decades ago.

Sex and anger are difficult for all of us to deal with. It helps to see them as primitive emotions designed to facilitate our survival. Keep these two principles in mind: Never forget where we come from (the jungle) and never forget what we are called to be (to transcend our biological foundation and aspire toward full humanization, full personhood).

A Contemporary Problem

Another issue arising of late is crippling people as prior struggles with sex and anger did. This is shame. Too many of us come into adulthood with a sense of self that has shame marbled through it, a pervasive feeling of self-defect, that we are inadequate in some fundamental way. If you would describe yourself as being perfectionistic, having feelings of inferiority, often pretending or making up stories about yourself to impress others, being defensive, needing to prove yourself or easily embarrassed, living your life as if playing to an audience, you have a heavy dosage of shame within your self-concept. It will take its toll.

Shame is not the same as guilt, even though we can feel both over the same action. Although a small amount of shame is not harmful, guilt is healthy and growth-producing. Our capacity to feel guilt makes us more human, giving us strength of character. Shame serves socialization purposes, whereas guilt ennobles us, helping us be moral in the face of opposing social forces.

We feel guilt when we violate the principles we choose to live by, when we are not who we want to be. Shame, on the other hand, occurs when we are not the kind of person we think *they* want us to be—whomever *they* happen to be. With guilt there is no move to secrecy, since we (or God) already know that we did wrong. But shame always leads to secrecy, because the feeling comes with the fear that *they* will find out who or what we really are.

Guilt always concerns behavior. We can do something about it by not performing that behavior, or doing what needs to be done to rectify the effect of the behavior. If we take an item from a store without paying for it, we feel guilty because stealing is something we consider wrong. We control the guilt either by not stealing, or paying the dollar value of the item to the store. Shame, on the other hand, is not action-connected but being-connected; it is not that we did bad, but that we are bad.

With shame, the only relief is death. Our language reinforces this: "I was so ashamed I could have died"; "I wished the ground just opened up and swallowed me"; "I wished I could have disappeared into the woodwork." Even the use of the word "mortified" to describe extreme shame connects it to death (*mors* is Latin for death). There is nothing you can "do" with shame. It traps you into secrecy, and you must commit more and more of your energy to supporting the secret.

Because shame is so painful we will endure almost anything rather than experience it. How many avoid discussing potentially lethal conditions with their physicians because they would be embarrassed (ashamed)? How many suffer great financial loss because they are too ashamed to expose their victimization, or suffer in silence and aloneness because shame keeps them from talking to a friend?

Shame is a powerful controller of human behavior, but it does not serve us well. Some years ago, I was speaking to an audience of clergypeople. During the break, a bishop came up to speak to me. One of his clergymen had made an attempt at suicide a fortnight ago by ingesting almost 100 aspirins along with a not-inconsiderable amount of alcohol, a lethal combination. Death was avoided by the quick response of an associate who induced vomiting and rushed him to the emergency room.

The attending physician, who happened to be a parishioner, wrote up the incident as an accidental overdose, thus avoiding embarrassment for the church. As a result, the man received medical treatment, but not the psychiatric attention he really needed. The bishop knew the truth from the associate, and his concern for a brother outweighed any threat of scandal. He asked that if the minister was willing to talk to me, would I do my best to be of help to him?

When I first met this 38-year-old man, his manner was deferential. He appeared overwhelmed by the seriousness of what he did, but uncomprehending of what led him to it. This was his first attempt at suicide, although the thought had intruded into his mind several times in the past. He believed suicide to be morally reprehensible and could give no adequate reason for his performing such a drastic act. He hypothesized, blaming the "evil one" who prowled the world whispering sinful ideas into the ears of the innocent. This man did not strike me as an evangelical fundamentalist, and my hunch was he knew more about where these thoughts came from than he was letting on.

Allowing his story to unfold was not profitable, as it moved away from self-revelation to a more neatly packaged accept-ability. Since he had a strong character structure and seemed to feel positively toward me, I moved to a more challenging, probing, and confrontational approach. This was not easy. The picture that came forth was deeply embarrassing for him to let out, as there was such a drastic split between his private and public selves. This split was such a severe source of shame for him that death seemed the preferable escape, offering both relief and atonement.

His shame focused on his sexual orientation. At first unsure what his orientation was (unusual for a man of 38), under aggressive probing it became clear that heterosexual attraction was minimal. He was deeply shamed about being homosexual, with even deeper shame around his activity. He would travel to distant cities where he would not be recognized, and browse gay bookstores hoping to make an anonymous homosexual encounter. After such encounters, he felt intense shame and guilt, and would resolve to never let this happen again. Then the next irresistible impulse hit him and off he was to another city, another bookstore, and another anonymous liaison. He was also a compulsive user of homosexual erotica, which shamed him even more than his anonymous activity.

None of this spilled into his professional life. He was a well-regarded clergyman, active in his community, and vehe-mently denied (and I had no reason to doubt him) ever violat-ing his professional responsibility by having sex with anyone with whom he had a pastoral connection.

There were other sources of shame which unfolded as time went on. There was shame around his motivation for entering the clergy; he saw it as a way of being asexual since his denomination found celibacy acceptable. He had a great rage toward the God who had made him this way and who turned a deaf ear to his pleading prayers to be other than what he was. There was shame in coming to grips with his masochistic and sadistic sexual fantasies. Possibly his greatest shame was around his own sexual molestation as a preteenager by a 17-year-old babysitter, the proverbial girl next door who was able to convince him that their numerous erotic encounters were his fault.

This man's sense of self was so shame-based that it was impossible for him to find his own way to any sense of personal self-acceptance, or any sense of being acceptable to others. He was not only to be despised by mankind, his behavior condemned him to eternal damnation, and thus his despairing hopelessness.

The minister's way out of shame was slow. As he began to face his shame, he found it necessary to sit with his bishop and discuss both his private life and his public one. The bishop's understanding, compassion, and patience greatly facilitated his ability to accept his own interior sexual pattern, which was furthered when he was able to find acceptance from his parents after telling them. As his self-disowning lessened, there was more integration of the masochistic and sadistic components of his sexuality, and he was finally able to form a relationship with another wherein his sexuality found expression. In time he was able to make a re-evaluation of his ministerial commitment, resulting in a more mature decision about how he wanted to live his life.

As the energy committed to hiding his shame and living a double life was freed up, he was able to use it for those things which gave him greater satisfaction. Shame had crippled him; until he was able to come to terms with it, his life was doomed to suffering.

A Common Experience

That so many of us are overburdened with shame is understandable. As we were growing up, shame was often used to force conformity. When we were told by our parents and teachers "Shame on you!" or "I am so ashamed of you!" or "You should be ashamed of yourself!" or some such statement, shame was being used to bring about desired behavior to shape us. It has always been a potent motivator, widely used, with unanticipated damage.

The kind of shame that we have so far focused on is a personal one, a chronic, gnawing sense that somehow we are defective and we must keep it hidden, because unless others think well of us, we will be outcasts. There is another kind of shame that, although painful, can be growth producing. It usually happens when we get a sudden insight into ourselves that gives us that "how could I have been so stupid" feeling and opens up a new, more satisfying, way of being. It is the essence of the "Aha!" moment in psychotherapy; it happens when you listen with sincerity, or when you permit some experience to affect you. All transformative moments, such as a conversion experience or a humbling encounter with another, involve this kind of shame.

We must recognize our own incompleteness in order to fully enter into a relationship with another; we must have a sense of our own sinfulness if we are to respond to what religion has to offer. This recognition, acknowledgment, or sudden insight all entail shame, frequently loaded with pain. It has the potential, however, to move us to a deeper level of experience. In that process of becoming different, we leave the shame behind.

If we have an excess of personal shame, then we are unable to experience this insightful shame. Not being able to

recognize or acknowledge any deficiency or defect in ourselves, the need to protect our fragile self-esteem precludes
being able to acknowledge anything negative. Personal shame
forces conformity, rather than transformative self-understand-
ing, and it interferes with our capacity to experience the kind
of shame that is a sincere acknowledgment of human authenticity.

Groups, whether the larger groups of societies and ethnic-
ities, or the smaller ones of employees, clubs, or social organizations, can impose an especially pernicious kind of shame on
its members. Both our need for bondedness and capacity for
shame are so great that groups can inflict significant crippling
on members through stigmatization. If our race, nationality,
age, sex, sexual orientation, disability, economic status, religion, or the like are explicitly or implicitly looked down upon,
we are stigmatized by a condition beyond our control.

In the late 1950s, I was a beginning teacher in a high school
in New York City, a school with only a small number of
African-Americans and Hispanics. The staff, as well as the
prevailing atmosphere in the school, was Caucasian. This was
before any significant civil rights legislation, and there was little sensitivity to a racist climate that was implicitly sanctioned.

On the first day of the fall semester, all students were
required to fill out identification cards. One of the questions
they were asked was about their race. What struck me at the
time was the number of African-American freshmen who
identified themselves as "American Indian." The prevailing
ethos—that everything good/beautiful was white, and everything bad/ugly was black—made these 13- and 14-year-olds
ashamed of their racial identity. They were trying to be white
or, if that was impossible, to be "next best" which was
American Indian. (The Indian, at that time, was seen as the

noble savage, given even greater nobility through his association with the white world). Schools, television, movies all held up the white culture as normative and judged all others relative to it. Being black was a stigma, a source of shame.

This same kind of stigma is felt by other minorities; it is felt by those whose nationality or religion is negatively stereotyped or whose sexual orientation is seen as a "disease." It is known by those who, because of their sex or their age, are excluded from full participation in groups or society. When someone is fired from their job, deemed to be unemployable, the recipient of public assistance through welfare, or is economically poor, society's perception of them as inferior inculcates a negative self-view. All those whom society places on the fringe can experience a subjective sense of shame.

The most deleterious effect of prejudice is not the negative consequences of resultant discrimination, but that the one discriminated against comes to believe there is truth in the prejudice. They come to believe they are defective people, not as good as those others, ashamed of who or what they are.

Although pernicious, this kind of shame can become a source of strength and growth if it mobilizes anger toward the holders of the prejudice and instills pride. Nothing bonds more quickly than a common grievance and identifiable enemy, thereby giving people the strength of character to refuse future victimization. When this is successful, we can see a sense of pride in the previously despised affiliation, such as in the "black is beautiful" and "gay pride" positions.

This stigma shame needs to stir up anger if it is to lead to a sense of self-pride. However, a group that may have an especially difficult time is a sub-group of the group that is looked down upon. Those who are rejected by their own minority group because they may exaggerate features of that group, or because they are perceived to embody the prejudicial stereo-type, are especially hurt. They may have no place as others move to a position of bonding and pride. If they bond to those with similar characteristics, they experience the rejection of both the larger group and the dominant society. This shame merges with self-shame and, because it is often difficult, if not impossible, to keep hidden, condemns its victims to an oppressive psychosocial crippling.

Not all shame need cripple. There is some shame that can be liberating; it may also be necessary in order to facilitate smooth functioning in our overcrowded and depersonalized society. Shame makes us behave in ways that are not unduly offensive or distasteful to the people that we encounter in our day-to-day living. A certain amount of conformity to the social niceties is necessary for living together harmoniously.

There are two things that can be done to find some freedom from gnawing personal shame. The first is to become aware of where our shame lies. We spoke previously of Carl Jung's the-ory that all of us have a shadow side containing the opposite of what we present to the world. The kind, gentle, compliant, pleasant man has an angry, aggressive, rebellious, abrasive side usually kept well hidden, even from the man himself. Whether we conceptualize in Jungian terms or not, we all have the full array of human emotions and behaviors, at least potentially, within us: Nothing human is alien to us.

However, this need not be any great problem. In Jungian thought, the shadow is only dangerous if we are unaware of it. Being aware of our potential for evil actually decreases the likelihood of it being acted on, and enhances the quality of our good. If we lacked any capacity for evil, our virtue would lose its luster, becoming "easy virtue," an unnuanced reflex, unidi-mensional and boringly dull.

We defuse shame in the same way, first by becoming aware of what it is that shames us. Usually we can tell where shame lies through those aspects of ourselves that we tend to be less than candid about, for example, our age, our nationality, our family of origin, our sexual orientation, our fear of professional incompetence, or whatever it is that is a source of embarrassment to us. The lies we live or tell point to fear, be it the fear of punishment or, more likely with adults, the fear of embarrassment or humiliation if the truth were known. What we uncover may not be the central core of the shame, but there may be no further need to know our deep, unconscious anxieties. Confronting the surface fears lessens the unconscious anxieties. Going back to the example of the minister, in peeling away the shames that we can identify we may get rid of the shames we cannot.

After we identify where our shame lies, the second requirement is to resist indulging it. We indulge shame by giving in to it, by permitting the lie to stand. If our shame lies around our age, every time we are less than candid about how old (or young) we actually are, we indulge the shame and thereby make it stronger. Whether we indulge directly, for example, by telling an age that is not true, or indirectly, by letting an impression stand that is not true, we have just strengthened our shame.

When we speak and live in truth, simply refusing to lie, we weaken the shame. No one does this perfectly; sometimes we may need to go back and correct a misimpression. What is necessary is that the effort to always stand in our own truth be a goal to strive for.

We experience a great sense of freedom when we discover that shame is gone, when there is nothing about ourselves that we would not share with anyone. This does not mean that we *do* share everything with everyone; not everyone cares to know everything about us. Also, there may be things about ourselves that others are not able to hear, and we may leave ourselves unnecessarily vulnerable to exploitation or abuse. But, our reason for not sharing is in the other, not because we would be too ashamed. The sense of personal liberation arises because now there is nothing about you that must be kept hidden. All you need to do is be who and what you are.

Getting rid of shame is a process, not done by a simple act. We may see it as not possible because the price we would pay for exposure would be too great. That may be understandable, but then we are stuck with the burden of shame. Is the onus of living with shame really more tolerable than placing your relationship or image at risk? It may take time and effort, but each step toward exposing shame is a step toward a healthier psychological life.

Questions for Discussion

1. Make a list of the 5 things about you that cause you to feel shame. Ask another to do the same, then exchange your lists and discuss them.

2. For everyone to like or admire us is imprisoning. It destroys our authenticity by forcing self-compromises. What we hope for is that a few people whose opinions we value will like and admire us. Who are those people whose good opinion of you is important? Whose esteem you value? Who is on your list that should be kept there? Who should be taken off the list?

3. What is your major secret? What is there about you (or your history) that you would be most ashamed of if it "got out"? Is there someone you could tell this to? Remember, we do not own secrets—they own us. What would it feel like to experience the freedom of living with no secrets?

4. If our sense of self is shame-based, much of our energy is used up in keeping ourselves hidden from the scrutiny of others. What did you learn from this chapter about shame and the ways to get free of it?

CHAPTER 6

ACHIEVING ADULTHOOD

Rituals are psychologically important to our sense of self. They provide confirmation of who we are, our status and person-hood, and facilitate our being able to incorporate new "selves" into our self-perception. The swearing-in ritual when we enter the military makes us, psychologically, a soldier; initiation rites make us a member of the sorority, club, fraternity, lodge, or institution; religious rituals make us one of the community or denomination.

There are rituals for entering or leaving employment that make us (or unmake us) part of an organization. Rituals sur-rounding birth, marriage, and death mark significant life tran-sitions for both the individual and those around her or him. Throughout life, rituals note beginnings and ends, confer status and power, reinforce meaning and authority, and act as signs along the way telling us who, what, and where we are.

At one time, all societies ritualized the important transition from childhood to adulthood. Traditionally, a boy or girl at the age of puberty was isolated from society, made to endure some testing of strengths or skills, and then re-admitted into the society with a new status and identity as an adult man or woman.

Western culture, by and large, has lost this transition ritualization. Bar mitzvah, bat mitzvah, and confirmation may represent religious adulthood, but do not affect adult sociocultural status in the secular realm. As a result, we have no clear demarcation points formalizing where childhood ceases and adulthood begins, and have created an artificial stage of development—adolescence—to fill the gap.

Although it is clear when adolescence begins (at puberty), there is no criteria for when it ends. Marriage once signaled adult status, but no longer; many postpone marriage to a later age or choose not to marry. To further complicate the picture, some embrace one aspect of traditional adulthood (parenthood) while rejecting another (marriage); others form a couple-commitment while rejecting the ritualization (legal marriage ceremony). Additionally, what is the status of the adolescent who marries or becomes a parent, yet still remains economically dependent?

Another possible criterion for adulthood is economic self-sufficiency. Once one takes responsibility for their own support and care, they are considered an adult. But what about those who move into their 30s and 40s still dependent on parents or society for economic assistance? They may never become self-supporting; does this mean they are never adults? You also have people who, for reasons of education, remain dependent on external support for a number of years beyond the age for assuming adult responsibility. We would be loath to call a 30-year-old postdoctoral student an adolescent, yet he or she may fail to meet the criteria for economic self-sufficiency.

What about using "legal age" as a critiera? Does becoming 18 or 21 years old automatically confer adult status? Hardly. The law has set arbitrary ages, varying from jurisdiction to jurisdiction, which are nothing more than legal conveniences for permitting rights and imposing responsibilities.

The real issue for psychological wellness is the need for an inner sense of being an adult. If we fail to achieve this, we find ourselves feeling like a non-adult inside an adult's body, with an intense fear of failing at adult tasks.

I have encountered numerous clients who have this particular fear. One was a successful business woman whom others admired as competent, capable, and reliable. Every morning, as she awoke and prepared for work, she experienced terrible anxiety, suffering from early-morning sweats. She could barely hold down breakfast, and had bouts of urgent diarrhea during the forty-minute commute to work.

Although she received a great deal of affirmation from her bosses and co-workers, inside she felt like an incompetent sham who, sooner or later, would be exposed. The woman lived in terrified anticipation of this exposure, and was unable to enjoy any satisfaction from the high quality of her work. She was genuinely surprised when others saw her as adult, because she saw herself as a child. Psychologically, she never transitioned into adulthood, even though her physiology did.

Although this woman may be an extreme case, many people suffer lesser versions of this same malady. Achieving a sense of adulthood in a society that does not overtly ritualize this transition is difficult.

The Adult as Male or Female

Our sense of adulthood is always anchored in gender. There is no such thing as an androgynous adult; we are either man or woman. A man's sense of adulthood is tied to feeling adequate in his maleness, that he able to fulfill his sociocultural role as man, that it is good to be a man and he is happy with his gender identity. So, too, a woman's sense of adulthood is always as woman. When we are deficient in this area we can have a sense of not being the man or woman we ought to be, and need to have our maleness or femaleness overtly affirmed by others.

Society and culture, to a large extent, define what is masculine and feminine. What is male and female is biologically based—genitalia, body morphology, some emotional and cognitive patterns, and certain behaviors. What is masculine and feminine in us, however, is psychological, learned through cultural and social expectations. What makes a man a man or a woman a woman is an inextricable blend of nature and nurture, the relative contribution of each being unclear at our present state of knowledge.

It is imperative to healthy adult development that we learn appropriate sex-role behaviors. This is as true in cultures that do not make a sharp distinction between appropriate behavior for men and for woman (the case in North America today) as in those cultures that *do* make clear what is permitted for each sex (the Islamic fundamentalist countries, for example). To feel adequate as a man or woman we must know what is expected of us. We may recognize the prejudicial factors in such expectations, reject the stereotypes, and push for greater gender equality; in so doing, however, our goal should not be to attain androgynous adulthood.

For many of us, it was our same-sex parent who welcomed

us into adulthood. At some point in our late teens or 20s, our fathers (for men) and our mothers (for women) went through some act, gesture, or words that acknowledged our new-found status as man or woman. It is likely that few of us were conscious of the ritual or the symbolism of this action, but we were transformed by it, and it enabled us to see ourselves as no longer a child. This ritual action—although informal and probably unconscious—admitted us into adult status.

Let me illustrate a few of the ways that this happens. When a mother holds her daughter's child—or a father, his son's—in her arms, and looks on her daughter with loving admiration, it acknowledges that you are a mother like she is a mother. Or, when a father notes his son's status as a profes-sional—likewise, a mother for her daughter—he clearly con-veys his regard for the son's achievement at becoming self-suf-ficient; this welcomes him into adulthood. There are countless other gestures parents use to confirm us as independent and autonomous, ready to enter into a new phase in our relation-ship to each other.

This is the power that parents have. If they fail to acknowl-edge us as adults, and try to keep us a child, dependent on them, our self-perception as man or woman gets crippled. We can fail to live up to their criteria for adulthood if we do not marry, do not get our own home, or fail to engage in profitable employment. This can cause our parents to delay our commis-sioning into adulthood.

Nature is generous, however. It almost invariably gives second chances. If a stage is missed the first time, some event or occurrence often comes later that can compensate. So, too, with the psychological transition into adulthood. What can happen is that someone else—a mentor—transitions us into adulthood. Mentors are usually older, the same sex, and in the same profession or line of work as we are in and, through their recognition and admiration of us, give us a sense of professional or occupational competence.

Since having a role (be it of teacher, plumber, or psychologist, mother or father) is an important factor in our awareness of adult identity, the mentor, by affirming our role-competence, indirectly affirms our status as an adult. There is a potential liability here; if the role—teacher, psychologist, parent—is lost, the sense of adulthood and personal significance can get lost, too. But as long as one has the mentor-affirmed role there is no problem.

The ritual of achieving adult status is a necessary step in the process of authentication. If we can look into our own histories and see how this was achieved, it can make us more sensitive toward those whom we will parent or mentor. Confirming adult status is no small contribution to make in the life of another.

Questions for Discussion

1. What did your parents do to confirm your status as an adult? Do you still, at times, feel like a child playing at adulthood? What do you feel most unsure about adulthood?

2. What qualities do you like in the men whom you choose to be friends with? What qualities do you like in the women you choose to be friends with? Do you seek friends who are similar, complementary, or the opposite to yourself? What does all this tell you about yourself?

3. Who have been your mentors? How did they convey a sense of your own competence or significance? What was there about them that enabled you to be mentored by them? Have you ever thanked them?

4. What have you done for your children (nieces, nephews) to help them achieve a sense of adulthood? How have you taken on the responsibility to be a mentor to others?

CHAPTER 7

HOW THERAPY CAN HELP

I have been a practicing psychotherapist for some 30 years, and have learned a great deal from the people with whom I have worked. They were from all walks of life: policemen, teachers, nurses, clergy, business people, secretaries, plumbers, physicians, college students, psychologists, fathers and mothers, gay and straight, from a wide variety of ethnic and racial heritages.

Some came with anxieties, others with compulsions, obsessions, sexual disorders and dysfunctions, thought disorders, mood disorders, and behavior problems. Each came to therapy with different histories and environments, and left with their own outcomes from the therapeutic process. Yet with all these differences and diversions there remain three commonalties which prod people into therapy, and the success of the therapeutic process inevitably rests on these.

1. *People come to therapy because they are aware of unhappiness or pain in their lives.* No one enters therapy because they are happy. They enter because they recognize some pain in their lives, even if it is the pain of having a spouse nag about the need to see a therapist. Whether it is the presence of a noxious emotional state, or the absence of positive affect, the pain of it leads people to seek help.

In over two-thirds of such cases, the person is experiencing a depression, either a major depression (relatively short-lived, but recurrent and severe) or a dysthymia (relatively long-lived, with mild to moderate effects). Granted, depression is a complex interaction of physiological and psychological processes, and sometimes a low mood can be a symptom of physical dysfunction.

Yet in my experience, the majority of depressions arise because people are not living their lives as they should; they are doing something or being someone deeply contrary to their nature. For the most part, they are unaware of what they are doing to cause and perpetuate the depression: If they knew, chances are they would do something about it. Much of the process of psychotherapy focuses on helping someone understand what is missing from their life, or why it is missing. Once this has been realized it becomes relatively clear what should be done to alleviate the depression.

There are certain needs that all of us have, and if we fail to meet them, we suffer. This is obvious on a physical level; if we fail to meet our need for nutrition or rest, we suffer physical distress. It is not so obvious on a psychological plane because our environment, history, or conflicting needs cloud our awareness. It is easy for our lifestyle to become toxic, and when it does, depression is inevitable.

2. People in therapy have given up the elusive pursuit of normalcy. When people begin to take their life seriously, they give up trying to be "normal." Some come to this on their own, but with others it can often be very difficult. One reason is that the pressure to be normal can be overwhelming. This pressure begins in the adolescent stage, when one of the developmental tasks of adolescence is to become culturally normalized.

Part of the pathway into the adolescent's future is to feel that they have a place in the larger world, which entails meeting normative criteria (i.e., "I have become part of. . ."). Even though adolescents can seem rebellious, disruptive, and anything but normal, their behavior exists in the service of normalcy, albeit a norm of peers rather than of adults. For the teenager, to be "normal" is necessary in order to integrate a stable identity.

There is still strong societal pressure toward normalcy in adulthood. Even though a society may give lip-service to developing individuality, it better serves a society's purpose to have people as reflexive conformists, to adopt a norm. Societies, cultural and religious groups, families, and governments each have their own criteria for what is normal. The problem is that these criteria are all subjective, or serve purposes that may not always be in the individual's best interest.

In psychology, as in other scientific disciplines, the norm is a statistical term; it means average, the middle ground of a normal curve distribution. Psychologists can say what is "sick," and may even be able to label something as "healthy," but when they move to say what is normative, apart from statistics, they leave psychology and enter the realm of philosophy and religion.

Practically speaking, normal means "like everybody else." Would you really want to be like everybody else? Can you think of anybody who has done anything significant with his or her life whom anyone would regard as "normal"? I doubt whether high achieving, fully actualized people ever worry about "being normal." They are too busy being happy and pursuing their goals.

Too often I am asked the question "I think this... or, I like this... or, I feel this... Is that normal?" If the question comes at a social gathering, my response, given in a solemn voice, is apt to be, "Well, there are medications you might consider for your malady!" If this question comes in a therapy session, issues are raised around seeking to be oneself while striving to be "other than."

We all have to give up our adolescence to experience adulthood, and this entails a refusal to be tyrannized into normalcy. Adolescents conform to get acceptance; adults conform because they confuse acceptance with love, and pursue the former when what they really want is the latter.

3. People in therapy are willing to start taking responsibility for their own lives. Most of us resist self-responsibility. However, no one else can make you happy; it is each person's responsibility to do what he or she needs to in order to be happy.

Most people enter therapy with an unconscious wish that the therapist will take over their lives, tell them what to do, and make them happy; the pull of dependency is great. Of course, they would resist like mad if you actually took over and told them what to do; yet the desire is still there. The reality is that this wish is a siren's call to the destructive loss of our individuality.

A subtle form of dependency wish-gratification is seen in blaming the fates for our unhappiness. "If only I had different parents... if my mother was not so controlling... if my father was not an alcoholic... if I was of a different religion... nationality... race... sex... sexual orientation... if I had brothers rather than sisters... was not a first-born... was rich rather than poor... if I went to this school rather than that school.... We can spend all day thinking about all the "if onlys," and nothing will ever change in our lives.

There is not much choice about what is most significant in each of our lives: We do not choose our parents, sex, family of origin, race, nationality, or even, for the most part, our religion. All of these are givens. The real question is, What are we going to do with these "givens"?

We can compare our situation to a game of poker, where our only choice is how to play the cards we are dealt. Whether we win or lose depends on how we play what we have, not on how much we complain to the dealer. So, too, in therapy. At some point each person has to say "This is who I am, and this is what I am going to do." Ultimately, we have to take responsibility for bettering our own lives.

The Three Stages of Psychotherapy

The practice of psychotherapy proceeds through three stages, distinctly identifiable phases where the focus of the therapy shifts. These are not discrete stages, as one flows into the other without the previous stage being complete.

Stage 1: Discovering who we are

This is what we traditionally think of as psychotherapy, where the person speaks about their mother, father, early life, etc. It is imperative that we come to understand the effect our environment has had on us, how it has shaped us both for good and bad.

Our early life has left each of us with strengths and weaknesses, with talents and with liabilities, with wounds and fragilities; it is essential that these be understood and owned.

Going back to our metaphor of the poker game, we must pick up the cards and look at them; we would not think of playing them blind. So, too, with ourselves; we have to have an adequate amount of self-knowledge in order to live our lives intelligently. We cannot take control of what we do not understand.

The goal of exploring one's early life is not to place blame or criticism, but rather, to achieve understanding in order to live life more responsibly. Interestingly enough, much healing takes place through this process of understanding. Out of increased awareness we find acceptance, and out of this acceptance we find both gratitude and forgiveness for those figures of our past. Likely, they were far from perfect, but given the limitations their own history placed on them, they did the best they could. A therapist is not necessary for us to do this first-stage work. He or she only facilitates it, but the work itself is essential in order for us to move onto the second stage.

Stage 2: Recognizing the need to change

Out of our increased self-awareness come two additional insights. First, we begin to recognize those behaviors, attitudes, and cognitions that are defeating our attempts to live out our own life. These behaviors may also be hurting others in our life who we truly care about and do not wish to hurt.

I recall the woman who became aware of the pain in her marriage caused by unrealistic expectations. As a child, she had wished for a benevolent, adoring, and self-disinterested father, but he failed to meet these desires. She brought the hurt and resentment from her father's betrayal of her expectations into her marriage and pinned them on her husband. This woman had to work out the betrayal within herself before she could ever look at the man she married and evaluate the potential for happiness with him.

I also recall a man who was determined not to treat his children the way his father had treated him. In the process of trying not to be who his father was, however, he was failing to be the father he ought to be and could be. A fundamental task of psychotherapy is self-change, not other-change. All things being equal, we should attempt to change ourselves before solving problems by manipulating the environment, e.g., divorce, job change, or moving to a different part of the world.

The second insight that arises from self-awareness, and which at first seems contradictory to it, is an increased willingness to be nothing other than what or who we are. This means not trying to live someone else's life through our own existence, or striving to be a self that is unfaithful to who and what we are. To quote a cliché, "What I am is good enough, if only I can be that."

Once, a client of mine came into a session totally gray-haired, only a week since I had last seen him. I was quite alarmed, to say the least. No reason for alarm, though; the man had simply decided to cease dyeing his hair. To this man, dyeing his hair said something about him that was not true; part of his commitment to stand in his own truth was his desire to look his age.

This may seem to have been a small, possibly even insignificant matter; but in reality it was not. This man committed a major portion of his energy to creating a younger self, because he felt unacceptable as who and what he really was. This small act of age ownership was part of an overall transformative movement toward a more authentic existence. Permitting our own uniqueness to flower and grow is not only the way to inner peace and happiness, it also allows us the opportunity to make our own contribution to the world. It may take effort to discover our own life agenda, but it is ultimately much more satisfying to live out our own agenda than to try and live that of someone else.

To work with someone through these two stages of psychotherapy is no small achievement. Traditionally, at least, it would now seem as if the goal of therapy had been reached. In reality, however, stages one and two are processes that are never fully completed. To find out who we are is a lifelong process, and although we may know ourselves better than anyone else will ever know us, we remain a student in this regard, continuously discovering and being amazed at the person we are.

So, too, we forever struggle with our limits and liabilities, our strengths and vulnerabilities, resisting the temptation to be someone other than ourselves. After all, was this not what tempted Adam and Eve—the promise of being like God, of exceeding human limits, of being other than human? None of us is exempt from this original sin, and part of our humanness is to keep pulling ourselves back into our own self, therein finding our destiny and our delight.

Stage 3: Finding our spirituality

Although people may be satisfied following therapy or their own processes of discovery—after all they are less anxious, their depression is gone, they no longer feel at the mercy of their obsessional thinking or compulsive rituals, and their interpersonal relations are better—for many, this is not enough. There is the desire to go further, to get in touch with something beyond our day-to-day, human existence. Here we enter the spiritual realm.

Psychotherapy, when pushed to its limits, becomes a movement into the spiritual. Carl Jung saw this when he talked about his patients in the second half of life (over age 35) whose problem, ultimately, was their failure to achieve a religious outlook on life. Jung believed that this situation had nothing to do with a person's particular creed or church membership, but rather, was "the soul in search of its proper path." Although I personally find difficulty conceptualizing in Jungian terms (my training has been more traditionally psychodynamic and experimental/experiential), I, too, am drawn toward a deepening awareness of, and sensitivity to, a spiritual dimension in human existence.

I would hasten to caution about the need to separate spirituality from the religion. (By religion, I mean the denominational, creedal, and institutionalized expression of the relationship between the human and the Divine.) Most people understand the distinction, and one of the more significant movements of recent decades, concomitant with the self-help movement, is the gradual separation of spiritual concerns from religious ones.

Religions are intended to promote the spiritual life, and often do this quite effectively. Yet too often, ecclesiology overrides theology, with the end result of doctrinal recital and submission taking precedence over transformative awareness and confession. When this happens, religion hinders spiritual development, rather than facilitates it. One might be tempted to hang a sign over church doors: "Caution: Entering here can be hazardous to your spiritual health."

It has long been noted that people who continue in psychotherapy beyond symptom relief often abandon their religious affiliation. I believe this happens because one's long-held religious beliefs and patterns may have supported dysfunctional behavior and attitudes. Once these patterns are modified, there is no longer any basis for a religious connection. Many in psychotherapy, however, become more authentically spiritual and, more often than not, remain in their religious family, but, connected in a much different way.

In discussing these three stages I have described a psychotherapeutic process. This is really a journey of growth and development, however, that all of us can and must go through if we are to live our lives as fully as we wish. Whether we undertake this journey within therapy or on our own, it is to our ultimate benefit and enrichment to seek out the pathways that lead to a better life.

Discussion Questions

1. What aspects of your self do you hide in order to appear "normal"? What are your eccentricities? How can you turn these into a source of self-pride, rather than a means of embarrassment?

2. What falsity about yourself do you directly, or indirectly, perpetuate? Is this pretense really worth the price of full authenticity? Do you need others to admire you so that you can admire yourself?

3. What does it mean to commit yourself to wellness? How do you reconcile this to a need to be unselfish? Can you be unselfish while giving priority to your own well-being?

PART III

SPIRITUAL WELLNESS

CHAPTER 8

SPIRITUALITY

At one time, psychotherapists assiduously avoided discussing spiritual issues with clients. Spirituality was the domain of the priest, minister, or rabbi trained in theology and religion, and beyond the competency of one trained in psychology or medicine. Giving counsel in an area outside of one's competency was (and is) an ethical violation; besides, there were enough psychological issues to be concerned about to waste time venturing beyond one's area of expertise. In reality, however, as some people were bringing psychological struggles to their clergyperson, others were bringing issues of spirituality to their psychotherapist.

Today, psychologists, psychiatrists, social workers, and counselors are unable to avoid dealing with their clients' spiritual issues. Questions such as, "What meaning does my life have? How can I cope with the thought of my death? Why should I place another's welfare ahead of my own? and Why should I not end my life now?" are as likely to be raised with psychotherapists as they are with the religious professional. Focusing only on the psychological leaves one frustrated, feeling incomplete about the therapeutic process. Both psychotherapists and their clients must get into issues of meaning and value—which, by definition, take us into the realm of spirituality—in order to bring about effective healing.

Issues of depression, anxiety, sexual dysfunction, obsessions, and compulsions are frequently brought to the clergy. Yet more often than not, they have had some training—either in seminary, a pastoral counseling program, or workshops—to help them recognize both the psychological problem and their own limits in helping with it. Ministers are taught how to counsel and when to refer.

On the other hand, the therapist typically has no training in theology or spirituality beyond his or her religious upbringing. Rare is the graduate psychology department, medical school, or postdoctoral training program that offers a single course in spirituality (there is none I know of that offers any in theology). Nor are therapists instructed on when they can assist in spiritual matters, and when they should refer a client to another source.

The relationship between psychology and religion has often been a nonharmonious one. In addition to the traditional clash between scientific and religious cosmologies, there is a unique tendency for psychology and religion to view each other with mistrust, and not a little antagonism. The psychologist looks aghast at the religious professional who treats psychological distress with spiritual treatments; while the minis-

ter views with serious reservations the psychologist who con-
fronts all life struggles with a diagnostic mind-set.

Indeed, although both disciplines have historical reasons
to be suspect of the other, there is no real need for antagonism.
Neither psychotherapy nor religion can afford to ignore the
spiritual; both have insights to share in this regard. Religion
focuses on a concept of God for its understanding of the spiritual; psychology focuses on a concept of the person to understand the same issue. Psychology is neither atheistic nor theistic; spirituality can be either. A therapist can be theistic or atheistic (or agnostic) and still have a well-developed spirituality.
Additionally, he or she can be quite facilitative of another's
spiritual quest, regardless of their own theistic stance.

Spirituality is too important for us to entrust exclusively to
religion. Religions, involved in their own institutional priori-
ties, often neglect or ignore what is needed to help people in
their spiritual quest. Without losing sight of the significant
contribution that religions have made to the world, they have
also contributed to war, human enslavement, gross injustices,
victimization, and dehumanizing practices. Too often religions
have been destructive to human spirituality. Part of the present disenchantment with religion, in spite of a simultaneous
intense interest in spirituality, reflects the failure of religions to
give priority to assessing and caring for the spiritual needs of
their people.

There is no argument that religions have a great contribution to make to human welfare as the custodians of a spiritual
heritage, but they too easily lose sight of their *raison d'être*
whenever a priority is given to some other interest. A personal incident recently captured this for me. While taking a walk
during a visit to New York City, I passed a large neo-Gothic
church. It seemed like a nice place to spend a few moments in

quiet solitude, away from the noise and bustle of the city. When I tried to enter, however, the main door was locked, as were the two side doors; it was 2:00 in the afternoon. The next morning, walking along a different street, I came upon another, smaller church; it too was locked up. Even the gate into its small outer garden was chained.

I am sure common sense dictated that these churches be locked: If they were open and inviting, all kinds of people could wander in. Street people might come in and sleep in the pews, even urinate in the vestibule; the smell of them would pollute the sacred atmosphere, and their presence discomfort parishioners. But would that really be so terrible? Could not the outcasts of society find something in space that belongs to God, even if it is only some warmth and dryness? What about thieves? Obviously, they aren't welcome. But, are the churches so concerned with protecting their material treasures that they close themselves to the needs of people?

Two days later, I was in lower Manhattan. Hoping to find something there, I went into the magnificent, historically significant Trinity Church at the head of Wall Street. This national treasure has plaques to mark where the Queen of England once stood, and presidents of the United States knelt. More than a monument, however, it was a place of reverential silence where one could pray, meditate, sit in solitude, or reflect on what really mattered in life.

There were street people there, likely in for the warmth and shelter; some were nodding into sleep, others stared into space, perhaps enjoying the interplay of color and stone, and others just sat lost in their own inner world. For the most part they were quiet, oblivious of others coming and going; perhaps there was even a thief among them.

This, to me, felt like a true house of God—open, welcoming all, receptive to the needs of the moment. It also was serving quite nicely as a place for prayer, meditation, or reflection for the many others who stopped in. I could not help but contrast this church to the locked and forbidden churches found on my previous walks, more concerned with protecting their space than with being places of refuge and sanctuary for the seeker.

As with the three-legged stool that does not work when one leg is missing, we need more than physical wellness and psychological wellness to be healthy; spiritual wellness is necessary, too. The insights of both psychology and religion have much to offer spiritual wellness. Very often, psychological awakening leads to a journey into the spiritual; it is this journey that I would like to reflect on.

What is meant by the term "spirituality"? I believe it is really a rather simple thing, possessed, often unwittingly, by people regardless of race, culture, education, intelligence, or religion. Spirituality is not something we acquire, rather, it is at the very core of our being, natural to us. If we endure an inconvenience to help someone in distress, sacrifice something of value in order to make another happy, or endure some pain to relieve another of a greater pain, we feel an enhanced sense of inner peace and personal satisfaction.

We, as a society, honor those who ignore their own safety and self-interest for the sake of another, make them heroes, give them medals, or build monuments to acknowledge their deed. On the other hand, we abhor those who refuse to assist another, or who never allow another's welfare to take preference over their own. This instinctive awareness in service to one another and to the common good is fundamental to the development of spirituality.

In its simplest terms, spirituality can be defined as whatever calls us to self-transcendence. It is that which motivates us away from self-focus or self-seeking, and inspires giving priority to the welfare of another. This can be a campaign or cause, like the pro-choice or pro-life movements, environmental causes, child welfare, world peace, or any involvement that calls us away from self-centeredness to the pursuit of a broader good. Causes are life-giving because of their capacity to bring transcendence; thereby, they birth a spirituality. (This, too, is what makes people vulnerable to cults; they offer a chance to forget the self and become totally absorbed in what is perceived to be a worthwhile endeavor.)

Religion offers a striving for self-transcendence through a response to the transcendent. Every religion can provide a spirituality, a belief system that can become the basis for self-transcendence and a systematic spirituality. Yet belief in God is not, in itself, spirituality. To believe in a transcendent being, or however God is conceptualized, is a hypothesis to explain the world, or to make it a safer place in which to abide. It is not, in a strict sense, a matter of belief, but rather, an intellectual or emotional explanation for existence. One can *think* of a supreme, omnipotent being as a plausible explanation for the origin of the universe; or one can *feel* the existence of God, a presence or sense that there is something "out-there." But this is not spirituality.

Spirituality begins when we respond to our hypothesis or hunch about a transcendent being. We begin to ask questions such as: What effect does my thought or feeling that there is a God have on my life? or, What search do I undertake after I intuit God's existence? The questioning process necessitates our creating an image of God to which we can then respond; this is the germination of a spirituality.

Each religion gives an image of God and elaborates appropriate responses. All religions begin as cosmologies, as attempts to explain existence and its consequences for humans, both individually and as a community. This is the essence of religion. For it to be effective as a source of spirituality, we have to make it our own, and assent to it in such a way that it makes us different from what we were before the assent. Thus, religion becomes the foundation of spirituality.

An affluent lifestyle and the acquisition of power are often the twin opposing forces to the development of spirituality. Both tend to become addictive; the more we have the more we need. We cannot imagine life without our possessions or power, and devote increasing attention and energy to sustain our lust. Ultimately, both fail to satisfy because neither leads to the sense of inner peace only self-transcendence can bring. Affluence and power both entrap us in self-centeredness; we end up powerless in the face of that which addicts us.

I am often pleasantly surprised by the depth of spirituality in some people, often those from whom you would least expect it. Simple people, without much formal education, often have profound levels of spiritual insight. On the other hand, I am often disconcerted by the lack of spirituality in those in whom you most expect it.

I have seen a deep spirituality in many clergy and others who make religion their career, but have also seen great deficiencies of spirituality in people of this same profession. Too many of those who make religion their business use it as business, becoming the sales force of doctrinal recitals or ecclesiological strictures. They fail to develop their own spirituality not only by succumbing to the twin temptations of affluent living and abuse of power, but by misleading those who come to them for true spiritual mentoring.

A Philosophy of Life

Our primary spiritual need is to have a philosophy of life that gives meaning and purpose to our existence, and helps us transcend narrow self-interest. In this, we have a sense of belonging to something larger than ourselves. This philosophy of life also becomes an integrating source when it operates as the principle around which we order our lives. To say someone is "well-integrated" implies that they have principles, values, or philosophies that determine how they live and express themselves.

How we conceptualize meaning and purpose can also become the foundation for the dream that guides our life. Although we may lose it along the way, each of us has a dream that becomes the central theme of our life drama; it is the beginning of the plot by which we live out the decades. If we are into or beyond the middle stage of life we can look back and see how our drama is unfolding. We can see how our life has been following along a pathway, and how both conscious decisions and serendipitous events fostered our movement along that pathway.

When we lose our dream, our life gets off track; subjectively, we feel discontent, malaise, or a sense of being endlessly stuck in our life. We may feel as if we are drifting like a rudderless boat. If we can reconnect to our dream, understanding its relation to what gives our life meaning and purpose, we experience a revitalization, a renewal of purpose in our life's journey. It may necessitate life changes to get us back on course, but these changes will be life-giving ones. Although having a philosophy of life that gives meaning and purpose is only the beginning of the process of spiritual growth, it is indispensable.

If we look at the major religions of the world—

Christianity, Judaism, Islam, Hinduism, and Buddhism—we see there are certain questions that each addresses. These questions arise in all of us, and are foundational to developing a spirituality. The answers vary from religion to religion, but the questions remain constant. At some point in our life, each of us has to face these questions and make peace with them. If we fail in this, we fail in our spirituality.

Every religion has an answer to life's basic question, "What is the meaning and purpose of our existence?" There are two other foundational questions, but before we look at these, let us consider the effect on us of religion's answers to these questions. Religions represent a potential danger to spiritual growth because they give us the answers to the deepest of life's challenges before we even ask the question. Therefore, they can deprive us of the greater profit which is in the asking.

God is not taught: God is discovered. (Or perhaps more correctly, God discovers us if we are seeking in the right place.) For our knowledge of something to be transformative, it must be generatively learned; the question must arise from our experience of living, and the answer generated from within that same context. This is not to say that the knowledge and experience of others cannot be helpful in the process, but this is facilitative assistance, rather than apodeictic. We must come to our own answer to the question if that answer is to have a transformative effect.

Answers abound to the question, "What is the meaning of our existence, the purpose of life?" If we accept one of the many available answers, the question no longer calls us to seek: We now have an answer. But if we choose an answer without deeply reflecting on why, it may not be an answer that will make us into a different person, that will be transformative. The question needs to be wrestled with, possibly tortured over. When we have an answer it may lack the surety of dogma, or the support of political consensus, but it will be ours alone, and we become different because of how we answered that question.

Most of us are taught a theology in early childhood. Parental figures, explicitly or implicitly, pass on to their children a meaning to life, which invariably has some transcendent dimension. Whether that transcendence concerns God or simply one's responsible connectedness to others, we are taught that our life has some meaning beyond ourselves. It is rare indeed that a child is raised to see that his or her pleasure is the sole purpose of existence.

This, then, becomes the basis of our childhood spirituality. As parents, our hope is to teach our children what will sustain them through life's journey. Yet it rarely works quite that way, because adults are always preparing children for a world they will never know. Our children will live in a world that we can't now envision, just as we live in a world unknown to our parents.

Of course, there are constants that do not change, but how do we know what they are, and how do we separate them from the peripherals that will lose their value? Concepts of God, morality, what constitutes responsible living, and the nature of spirituality are very different today than they were a half-century ago; the same for a half-century from now. Preparing children to be adaptable to a completely new genre of moral and spiritual issues is a daunting task, yet one that is essential to helping children successfully navigate their own life journey.

Too often, we get trapped in a concept of God that destroys the potential for in-depth spirituality. Usually, this concept comes from our childhood learning, since this is what becomes the basis for spirituality. If we are to grow we have to undo the images of God developed as children and reverse the learning process, so that our spirituality and concept of God grow out of our experience of life. In discovering God this way (or, in being discovered by God in our openness), our faith and spirituality can give new form to our existence.

As children, our spirituality was grounded on a theology, that is, an understanding of God and our relationship to this God. As adults, our theology must become grounded in our spirituality, in our experience of finding transcendence as we attempt to live authentically. We must learn to trust our experience to lead us to a new, possibly deeper, understanding of God even if it means rejection of all that we have learned before.

When people come to grips with meaning and purpose, God and spirituality, they are invariably moving toward a deeper level of existence, a more profound sense of inner peace and satisfaction. It is invaluable to have someone to companion us through this spiritual seeking. Psychotherapists may be the least helpful, because so many have not made the journey themselves. Clergy are a shade better, but only a shade since so many of them are administrators of "spiritual gas stations," rather than true soul guides.

In this regard, spiritual directors are becoming recognized professionals, trained specifically to facilitate spiritual growth in others. Clergy and non-clergy are recognizing the need for training in spiritual direction in order to assume this role, and programs that provide such training are proliferating. It is interesting that this profession is growing so fast at this time, often independent of formal religious organizations. To me, it speaks of the spiritual hunger that so many are experiencing, and of their looking beyond institutional religions to satisfy this yearning.

It may be a bit misleading if it seems that I am presenting the task of finding a philosophy of life as a constant source of peace and happiness. Although this task is foundational to a satisfying life, it can also leave us open to some painful experiences. Sometimes I believe it would be easier to have an unquestioned, unchallenged, authoritative religious faith that provides a recipe for living without doubt or searching. This is part of the appeal of fundamentalist religions. Their literal acceptance of authoritative faith-teachings and noncomplex views of spiritual authenticity give followers an enviable sense of surety. This is very appealing when "dark nights" cloud our vision and we walk with fear and trepidation through days of spiritual discouragement and failures.

I have worked with clients whose simple faith sustained them through difficulties. However, there were many others whose faith was imposed from outside themselves, affirmed by an authority, unscrutinized and unchallenged by experience. Theirs was a spirituality that was not liberating, or welcoming to broader experiences; rather, it constricted them and limited their response to life.

A man in his middle thirties came to therapy because of sexual difficulties. He was a high school biology teacher, unmarried and living alone, at some distance from his family. All his socialization took place within his church; in fact, he lived his life between the two parameters of school and church. He was a nonactive homosexual, reporting some same-sex exploration with an age-mate when he was 13 years old, but never any sexual experiences since that time.

Several of his students, as well as a younger man in his parish, had become a source of obsessive erotic fantasies for this man, resulting in an irresistible urge to masturbate. In his mind, committing a homosexual act was too reprehensible for him to even consider actually indulging his fantasies with another adult. The shame he felt for "what he was" caused him considerable personal distress. He came to therapy seeking a cure for his homosexuality, his uncontrollable thoughts, and his masturbation. All of these were severely proscribed by the teachings of his church, which saw any sexual act outside of marriage as gravely sinful. Homosexuals were especially condemned.

His situation presented a dilemma. Since neither homosexuality nor masturbation is a disease or illness (mental or physical), any attempt to "cure" this man through therapy not only had little chance of success, but could actually cause harm. It also raised an ethical question, the same as if a physician attempted to cure left-handedness or blue eyes. Under different circumstances, a reasonable therapeutic approach would likely focus on his inability to accept and integrate his sexual orientation into his life, and address the guilt and shame he felt about sexual expression. In this case, however, the man's dogmatic religious beliefs about the "evil" of his sexuality made minimal the likelihood of change with either of these therapeutic approaches. Additionally, failure to respect someone's religious beliefs raises ethical issues for many therapists, myself included.

Therapy can help to make sexual expression more relational by addressing fears and anxieties concerning intimacy and being sexual. As his sexual shame decreased, the man could have allowed himself to express his sexuality with someone for whom he felt affection, respect, and some degree of commitment. But this man wanted to be rid of *all* sexuality, even though his previous efforts toward being asexual were a failure, and made him miserable. I did not want to be party to helping him toward his unrealistic goal.

After explaining what I could offer by way of assistance, he decided that psychotherapy was not for him. An alternative, and what would help him meet his goal, was to join SLAA (Sex and Love Addicts Anonymous) or SA (Sexaholics Anonymous). Both of these organizations use an addictions treatment model based on a 12-step approach, identical to the Alcoholics Anonymous (AA) approach to preventing alcohol abuse. The aim is to control sexual expression either by totally eliminating all sexual expression (SA) or permitting very limited sexual behavior (SLAA). The man opted to pursue one of these approaches, and I gave him the information he needed to make contact.

I do not know what happened to this man. I wish he could have become more open to accepting his sexual orientation, thereby finding growth and a sense of pride in himself. If he were more accepting of himself he would find it easier to control his sexual behavior, bringing it in line with legal, social, personal, and religious expectations, which is something we all must do. Actually, his homosexuality had the potential to be a significant positive force in his life. The capacity for love and caring in many gay and lesbian people can surpass what is found in the straight population. For many homosexuals, there is often a profound awareness of the spiritual dimension to life, an attraction toward religion, and a deep sensitivity to communal responsibility. These are qualities our society sorely needs.

Our sexual orientation is as intimate a part of us as is our race or nationality. If it is a source of negative self-evaluation, we severely hinder our capacity to live a meaningful and satisfying life. Also, disowning our sexuality affects our capacity to transcend the self, as this transcendence, the essence of all spirituality, presupposes self-acceptance. What brings us to spirituality is not an escape from a despised self, but rather a vision of something greater than self that incorporates both who and what we truly are.

Questions for Discussion

1. What in your life calls you to self-transcendence? What did you learn from this chapter that was helpful in your own search for self-transcendence?

2. What role does religion play in your spirituality? What religious experiences have helped your spiritual life? What experiences have hindered your spiritual life?

3. What "philosophy of life" gives a meaning and a purpose to your life that helps you transcend narrow self-interest? What forces hinder you from living in this "philosophy," and pull you back into narrow self-interest?

4. What event(s) in your life brought you to face the question of the meaning and purpose of your life? Did what you learned in your family, church, or school help in your struggle to confront this question? Have you ever really confronted the question?

CHAPTER 9

EVIL

All those whose life philosophy posits a Higher Being, an intelligence guiding the universe, are brought face-to-face with perhaps the most difficult dilemma facing a believer. The way we deal with this fundamental issue comes from the depths of our lived experience, and is known as *theodicy*. Literally translated from its Greek roots, theodicy means "God's justice." Practically speaking, a theodicy is an explanation of why a God who is just (and all the major religions of the world, Christianity especially, describe God as just) allows evil to exist.

When evil ones get their "just deserts" we are tempted to applaud, because that is the way the world is supposed to operate. The scales of justice are balanced and the world makes sense to us. However, when a loved one dies needlessly, or a tragedy

119

strikes suddenly, when it is the good who are made to suffer and the evil seem to triumph, the unavoidable question "Why did God let this happen?" arises from the crushing pain in our soul. It is nearly impossible to look at the Holocaust, or other cases of the brutal, systematic slaughter of people and not ask the question: "Where was God?" If the God we worship is benevolent, omnipotent, and just, then why do innocent, decent, powerless men and women experience so much pain and suffering? This is the dilemma inherent in theodicy.

All religions see God as having omnipotent power and as being benevolent toward humans, caring for and about them. Why, then, is there so much innocent human suffering? If we did evil, or were evil, we could understand the need for suffering to serve justice or teach us the error of our ways. But when people who are not evil, who are virtuous and do only good are the suffering victims, while those who are evil prosper, we ask "Why?"

Some maintain that religions begin in the attempt to find answers to these questions; I doubt that. Religions begin as attempts at understanding, explaining, and predicting nature, as hypothetical explanations of where we come from, why we are here, and where we are going, a means to make some sense of ourselves and the world we live in. By making our world understandable, it becomes predictable and we feel more secure in it. Science does the same thing, except its hypotheses are testable, where those of religion are arational and transmitted through myths.

On the other hand, the problem of evil makes people leave religion more often than any other. Every religion attempts to answer the question of why there is evil in the world, but, not infrequently, it is the answer that destroys faith when it proves inadequate to the experience of the sufferer.

All people must question God's justice if their potential for spirituality is to be expanded. Although these questions are frequently discussed with the clergy, they come up in psychotherapy, as well. When the therapist responds in a way that focuses on the question rather than on solutions, when the therapist permits the question to sear the soul of the client and avoids offering pat answers, it can be an occasion for growth. Therapists can sometimes be in a better position to prompt a spiritual response than could a clergyperson since he or she is not bound within a religious tradition offering dogma-based responses.

All religions have an answer to why God allows evil, but often, one religion's answers are at variance with the ones offered by others. Some religions find an answer in increasing adherence to the will of God in the face of our inability to make sense of suffering. Others see all suffering as temporary, balanced with rewards in an afterlife. Still others see the world as a battleground between God and the devil, between good and evil, with the latter the source of suffering and the former, ultimate triumph. Some find an answer in believing that the nature and extent of human suffering proves there can be no God, or that if there is a Supreme Being, then God is unworthy of human recognition, never mind worship.

Some say that evil and suffering are for our ultimate good, trying to teach us lessons that we need for salvific profit. Others say that none of us is innocent, that we are all guilty of sin and deserving of suffering; God's benevolence is shown in there not being more suffering. Some see the fault in ourselves, that we suffer because we expect or hope for something better; if we abandoned such hopes and expectations suffering would cease. Others see it as a way of teaching us hope. Some see life as a system of rewards and punishments, eventually balancing out in the scales of eternal justice. Christians find suffering redemptive in its bringing us closer to a suffering Savior.

A Tortured Life

Many years ago, I found an especially poignant response to evil from an older colleague, a kind, gentle man who radiated a serenity that drew others to him. This was a man whom you immediately sensed was holy, at peace with himself and with his life. I look back on him as a special kind of mentor. We met when we were both teaching at a small liberal arts college, I at the beginning of my career, he nearing the end of his. We spent many an hour in conversation on a wide range of issues, usually in the area of psychology, psychotherapy, or then-popular psychoanalytic theories.

The man never talked much about his own life. I knew only what was generally known about him, that he had emigrated to America from Poland after World War II, and had family over there but lived here by himself. Once when he reached for sugar for his coffee, I noticed fading tattooed numbers on his forearm, indicating that he was a survivor of the Nazi concentration camps, an experience he never talked about.

One evening, he phoned to say that he was ill, and to ask if I would proctor the exams for his course, scheduled for the next day. I agreed, and following the exams, brought the completed papers to his apartment. He answered my knock dressed in a ratty old sweater and baggy chinos, staring at me with rheumy eyes that hesitated in their recognition. After a moment he connected, and invited me into his kitchen. He offered me a glass of whiskey, the same as was in his own glass, already poured and on the table. I then realized that the "illness" that had kept him from proctoring his own exam was neither bacterial nor viral.

We sat at the kitchen table and talked; actually, he talked and I listened. It seemed that today was an anniversary for him, although he never said of what. His conversation was the most personal I had ever heard from him, as he spoke of his life in Poland. He told me of his father, who was a legal scholar and judge, his brother, a teacher, and his sister, a musician. He remembered his school days, how he met his wife and fathered two sons, and how good family life was, with many dreams for the future. Then the war broke out, and although this was 1965, 20 years since that war had ended, the events of those years were as vivid to him as if they had happened yesterday.

Being Jewish, life was not easy under the Nazi occupation in Poland, but the man was able to find some manual work and support his family. One evening, as he was walking home from work, he was conscripted into a forced labor battalion, simply picked up off the street. As he was put onto the back of a truck, he saw his wife and sons, 6 and 4 years old, for the last time; they had come to meet him that evening to accompany him the rest of the way home.

He survived the camps, but never said how. I sensed that this story was better left alone. He prayed passionately that his family members would survive, too; not a day went by that he did not plead with the God of Abraham, Isaac, Jacob, and Moses to spare his wife and children, parents, brothers, and sisters, from the horror he was seeing. He offered himself as a propitiation if only they survived.

After the war, he could find no trace of any member of his family—they seemed to have all vanished from the face of the earth. Overwhelming evidence suggested they were all murdered, but he could find no records to verify this. Numerous attempts to find answers through various relief agencies and correspondence with non-Jewish acquaintances in Poland all came up empty. Eventually, he gave up all hope of ever knowing what had happened to his family.

He was tormented, not so much by being robbed of his family, but by the thought of the suffering they may have gone through. Were his children the subjects of medical experiments? What abuse did his wife and sister have to endure, and what depredations were his father and brother subjected to? He knew what went on in Auschwitz, Buchenwald, Dachau: Did they die quickly and mercifully, or did they linger for months in inhuman conditions? Not knowing gave his imagination license to torture him.

Through all of this, God was silent. In his life before the war, the man had been an observant Jew, a student of the Talmud, one whose religion was more that just a source of identity. How could the God to whom he had been faithful done this? Yet no miraculous gift of merciful understanding was his, no Job-like thundering rebuke for his questioning: nothing, but silence.

What kind of God could permit this? The question gnawed at him incessantly. If only he could have given up belief; atheism would have been a relief for him. But his sense of God had too much psychic reality for him, and blocked him from being able to dismiss the Divine entirely from existence. He could not deny God, but he could refuse to show respect for any religious expression. He flaunted dietary prescriptions, ignored Sabbath restrictions, and never attended synagogue. If God existed, he hated this Being.

Finding Peace within Pain
After his arrival in New York, the expression of his hatred grew more intense. If an orthodox Jew sat next to him on the

subway, he would change his seat. He would turn his back on a Christian in clerical clothes. If asked what his religion was, he replied, "I have none." He took evening walks and, coming upon a church or synagogue, would find a secluded spot on the outside wall and urinate on the building. Spoken softly, but full of venom, he would say, "God, I piss on you!"

His expressions of rage offered him little relief. Psychologists talked to him about his guilt at surviving when all those he loved perished, but this only added fuel to his anger toward God. Friends offered the accepted dogmatic responses to his question, "Why?," citing God's respect for the free will of human beings, or that God's ways are unfathomable, or that God must have some purpose in preserving him, or similar well-meaning answers. Yet none of these held any hope for him: They were merely pietistic clichés, statements of exhausted creeds.

One pre-dawn morning, after another sleepness night plagued by angry thoughts, he walked the few blocks from his home to the harbor of Brooklyn Heights. As he looked over the dark waters, a lone tugboat was making its way across the bay toward Staten Island, its lights bobbing on the inky murk. Something inexplicable in the sight of this tug steadily holding its course as it passed beneath a silent, disinterested Statue of Liberty released a voice within him that cried out in pain, "God, I can't forgive you for what you did!"

Forgive God? He had never thought in these terms before. "Who am I to forgive God? It is God who forgives! And yet," he thought, "must I not find forgiveness for God?" It was at this moment that he found a way through his rage. He began to weep as he had never done before; his tears would not be silenced. As the sun rose over the harbor a few hours later, he remained seated on the same bench. The scene of the tug moving along the watch of the great statue symbolized something impossible for him to put into words. Was it the relative insignificance of such a ship, determinedly making its way across the water, its sole function to provide assistance to larger ships with important cargo to carry, that affected this man so profoundly?

Many people must have seen this man staring into the horizon from Brooklyn Heights that morning, for he did not leave that bench until after noon. He had found within himself the depth of character to offer God forgiveness. A deeper understanding came when he reached inward for the forgiveness, and felt something that he could only describe as God apologizing to him. No visionary image, no thunderous voice came forth, simply a sense of reconciliation and peace. Perhaps someday he will discover how it all came together for him, but that is not what is really important. What matters is that this was a transformative moment, a catalytic experience leading into spiritual release and new freedom. He was profoundly changed in this instant.

I wish I could say that he became peace-filled for the rest of his life, but this would not be true. Often a particular memory would tear at the old wound, and the pain would surface: seeing a young man of the same age his son would have been or a woman with the walk of his wife, or hearing a certain piece of music would make his eyes tear and his throat constrict. He would then pause and renew his forgiveness, reminding himself of how deep this forgiveness had to go.

I well remember his words as I sat with him that day at his kitchen table: "It is not easy to really forgive someone, especially God, and I have to repeat my forgiveness often. But, the more I do, the more aware I become that there are also things I am grateful for!" Both forgiveness and gratitude were important parts of this man's holiness, and of the gentleness and peacefulness that came to characterize him. This twentieth-century Job found an answer to the problem of evil, a task that each of us must undertake. At some point within the drama of our lived experience, we will each ask the question why and, if allowed to, will eventually discover an answer that will transform us.

Probably in no other area is the conflict between religion and life experience more pronounced than in addressing theodicy. Inevitably, each of us experiences the hurt, pain, loss, disappointment, failure, or injustice that leads to the "Why, God?" question. We must be free to find an answer to that question that is grounded in ourselves. The question, more than the answer, is the source of spiritual growth. Often I have sensed a deeper spirituality in those who genuinely reject a concept of God that does violence to their experience of life, than in those who have a blind submission to a concept of God that makes a mockery of their integrity.

I have often seen people find their way back to their inherited belief system, but who now see it in a totally renewed manner, able to make its wisdom their own. In the words of T.S. Eliot, they "see it again, for the first time." Others find new belief systems, or dispense with all systematic theological structures, finding instead a generative belief system that is sustaining. Some find their way through suffering, loss, disappointment, and unanswered prayers by forgiving God. Others through a belief in the meaningfulness of suffering. Still others find relief in submission to that which they do not understand, but which is their own.

"Solutions" to the problem of evil range from irreverent atheism through devout theism. Concepts such as the devil, original sin, matter as evil, doctrines of salvation and afterlife, grace, karma, the need to accept God's will, and the wish for permanence are all used to resolve the issue. So, too, are concepts of human self-sufficiency, randomness of events, and noncausality. Yet attempting to find a solution is an approach that may mislead. As intellectual descendants of Galileo, Newton, and Descartes we in the West tend to solve what we do not understand through rational discourse: We think in "cause and effect" paradigms. This is not the only way to understand the nonunderstandable.

Perhaps what we need to do is to know that we do not know, to simply understand that evil exists in the presence of good, that shit happens in the nicest neighborhoods. This is not irrational; it is arational, transcending the categories of our rational, cause-and-effect thought processes. Not all "problems" have "solutions"; some things are simply "realities." Is this what the Book of Job, this magnificent treatise on theodicy, is telling us? Job was an innocent victim whose only offense was that he was sinless. He could not explain his suffering, but rejected the dogma imposed on him by others, who told Job that evil was visited upon someone in retribution, to keep the scales of justice in balance. What Job teaches us is that the cause of innocent human suffering is not known by us; we only know that it exists.

My colleague's journey from pain and suffering, through anger and rage, rejecting easy answers and finding forgiveness within himself, led him to personal authenticity and a new connection to a transcendent vision of life. If he had accepted the comfort of a prepackaged solution, it may have stunted his growth. He needed to have his question sear his soul to cauterize his woundedness and permit new, healing growth.

This particular task in developing a spirituality—finding our own theodicy—follows once we have discovered that which gives meaning and purpose to our existence. This step of the journey may be more significant for the theist, but even those who do not believe in God still try to make sense of human suffering. Even if our intellectual explanation says that life is simply a series of random events, and that nature is indifferent toward pain and suffering, we can find a spirituality in the courage to face what life's random code places before us. Ultimately, all of us surrender to that which is beyond our ken.

Questions for Discussion

1. How do you reconcile the existence of innocent human suffering with the existence of a just, benevolent God? What events in your life led you to this question? What pathways did you follow to find your answer?

2. What did your family, or religion, teach you about why bad things happen to good people? Did this assist or hinder your own attempts at understanding why you were a "good person" to whom a "bad thing" happened? How?

3. To reject the comfort of the easy answer opens the possibility of spiritual growth. In light of what you read in this chapter, how does your understanding of this statement apply to your life?

CHAPTER 10

$\underline{D}_{EAT}\underline{H}$

In considering the spiritual journey, each individual must address several truths. These great truths, the *aeternae veritatis* of human existence, can be a source of great distress, what the existential writers and thinkers describe as the "dread unto death." Philosophers like Søren Kierkegaard, Martin Heidegger, and Gabriel Marcel; novelists like Albert Camus, Jean-Paul Sartre, and Simone de Beauvoir; and psychologists like Erik Erikson, Abraham Maslow, Carl Rogers, and R.D. Laing have, in the last century, sensitized us to these primal themes and to the difficulties they can cause throughout human life.

There are four generally recognized eternal truths. We will address each of these separately in this and the subsequent three chapters. Each puts us in touch with our vulnerability as humans like nothing else can. Countless cultural and religious myths offer solutions to the dilemmas these truths present, but these truths are not meant to be avoided, solved, or explained away. Rather, they are to be embraced and allowed to become part of our being. They are not problems to be solved, because they have no solution; when a problem has no solution it ceases to be a problem, and becomes a reality.

Because the great truths are so difficult to cope with, we use elaborate maneuvers to keep them at the edge of consciousness, away from full awareness. When blissful ignorance is impossible, we invent socially supported fictions or elaborate stories to keep truth remote. To accept the great truths in their naked rawness is often too much for us, since they cause such intense anxiety. So we salt them with fable and pour fanciful myths over them, making truth more palatable by dulling its reality.

If we reject ways of denying them, the eternal truths enrich our experience of life in the here-and-now, and carry us to deeper spiritual authenticity. Surrender to these truths, as paradoxical as it may seem, brings great inner peace. In embracing them, we come to find our experience of life deepened by an increased sensibility of what it means to be a human being, fully alive.

Issues surrounding the great truths, not unlike those of the problem of evil, inevitably arise in the context of people's lives. If these issues are raised during the course of psychotherapy, the task of the therapist is to discourage premature, unexamined, or obviously misleading solutions, encouraging a search for what helps make sense of the question. Every religion addresses the great truths, as well; the problem here, as with theodicy, is not whether the answer is true or not, but that we are given the answers before we ask the questions.

It takes courage to face these existential questions, to experience fully the terror that such questioning brings to us, and to let ourselves be transformed by an answer we can assent to. The effective psychotherapist or minister companions another along their inner journey, challenging the other to honestly face the questions, and bringing the individual to his or her own conclusions. For it is in generating the answer that we truly come to know it.

The first, and perhaps most obvious, eternal truth is the inevitability of our own death, as well as the death of those we love and cherish. Each of us is going to die, to lose everything that we have accumulated and all whom we have loved. Everything we have accomplished will be left behind. To the best of our knowledge, no one has escaped this fate. Death awaits each of us.

I am sure this does not come as a surprise to you. Of course we know that we are going to die, but are we really fully aware of it? Has it burned itself into our consciousness, so that when we look deeply into the eyes of a loved one—parent, spouse, child, grandchild—we feel a true sadness in the knowledge that we will eventually separate and lose each other? No matter what wealth we accumulate, position we achieve, or power we amass, death will take it all away. No matter what "monument" we leave behind, the memory of who we are eventually fades, and there will be no one left who knew or remembers the "me" we struggled to immortalize.

The North American culture offers little support for acknowledging the reality of death. Few of us have had any direct experience of death. Of course, we have all had the experience of someone connected to us dying, but the death itself was likely remote. Most people die in institutions, separated from their life companions. We may visit them in the hospital, nursing home, or extended-care facility, yet unless death strikes suddenly and unexpectedly, the rest of us are shielded from the actual events of the dying process.

Likely, the person will die in the presence of a professional caregiver—nurse, physician, chaplain, attendant—and the family receive the news by phone. When we finally see the dead person, it is usually when she or he is lying in the funeral home, all dressed up in her or his finest clothes, cosmetically made to look asleep, with no sign of the agony of death. All of this has the effect of making death less real for us, of denying its totality and permanence.

The euphemistic language used to describe death also takes the reality out of it. We speak of the deceased as "having gone to a better life," "finally at peace," in his or her "eternal sleep," "laid to rest," or other such phrases. We tell each other how good the deceased looks, and we comfort ourselves by saying that he or she "will be waiting for us in heaven." Though these sentiments may console the survivors, they detract from the reality of death by suggesting something other than the end of that person's life.

Unlike previous generations, our experience of death is mostly with the elderly. In 1890, 75 percent of all parents experienced the death of one or more of their children; today, this statistic is down to 17 percent. Because medical science has made the death of children a relatively uncommon experience, we tend to connect death to the aged. Perhaps this is why, especially in the North American culture, we try to distance ourselves from older people: They speak to us of mortality, a message we would rather not hear. We spend billions of dollars every year to look younger, to hide the fact that we are aging, getting closer to that barrier that separates life from death. Is it death we are hiding from?

It is interesting to contrast the way North Americans approach death with the ways of other times and cultures. Look, for example, at the amount of death and physical violence found on television programs and movies, our major cultural expressions. Our anesthesizing death by making it into entertainment is not dissimilar to what the Romans did in the early Christian era. Actors and actresses "die" for our pleasure, in a fashion no less dramatic than the gladiator losing his battle with the lion. But the actors go the gladiator one better by creating the illusion that death is not final, because they then appear, marvelously alive, in another film or television program!

Buddhism teaches that the primary source of all human suffering lies in the human desire and search for permanence. We want life to last forever, and hope for a timelessness in which there is no loss. Yet this desire goes against all principles of life, and therein creates the conflicts which cause suffering and pain. For the Buddhist, it is only by facing the truth of no permanence in this world that one can live in a more authentic way, fully in the awareness that all will come to end.

While living among an aboriginal tribe some years ago, I had the privilege of witnessing the death of a tribal member. The way in which the tribe dealt with this death had its roots deep in their history. All the members of the tribe were aware of the impending death and came to be with the dying person, making no effort at denial or blunting the reality that death was coming. Family and other tribal members were present to companion the dying member into the final journey. Grief was expressed openly, sometimes in an exaggerated manner.

After the person died, family members clothed him in a simple shroud, a garment worn only by the dead. An all-night vigil was held before the day of the funeral, in the tribe's assembly hall. Each tribal member who was able spent this night in the presence of the body, not so much to console the family, but as a demonstration of their solidarity in grief. During the funeral ritual, each tribal member came forth, embraced the body, and gave it a kiss of farewell. When the body was buried, life returned to its usual routine.

Monks and nuns in medieval monasteries kept a skull in their cells to remind them of the inevitability of death; it was a way of keeping their life in perspective. They tried to face life with death as an integral part of the picture, yet did not become morbidly gloomy or obsessed with death. Perhaps the epidemic of depression sweeping across North America is connected to our emphatic denial of death. An awareness of death, both our own and of those we cherish, that one day, both we and those we love will die, is foundational to wisdom, and makes rich the moments we now live. Acceptance of life's realities, one of which is death, leads away from depression into a greater sense of satisfaction, joy, freedom, and peace.

Death, Myth, and Denial

All cultures create myths about death. Even though most myths surrounding death contain beliefs of an afterlife, the basic intent of the myth must be to help survivors understand the meaning of death in relation to life, rather than provide consolation through the denial or avoidance of death. In order for myths to be effective, it is necessary for us to fully experience the death of another as it occurs, as well as face the inevitability of our own death. Otherwise, the myth will merely dull the reality of life's end.

Many contemporary myths surrounding death are found in children's cartoon shows. Children instinctively fear death, long before they have any understanding of it. This is why the truths a culture wishes to teach about death often show up in stories for children.

Cartoons give a clear message about death, one which viewers may not be distinctly aware of. In these stories, humanized figures get killed over and over again; yet they always come back, none the worse for the experience of dying. The essential quality of death, its permanence, is ignored. To the best of my knowledge, the folk tales of no other culture deny death as we do, but give it its place within life.

Are we perpetuating a system of denial because we refuse to face the reality of our own death? Previous generations created euphemistic myths around sexuality, because at one time we were ashamed of our sexual needs, desires, and activities. Yet becoming aware of how destructive these myths were, we now teach children the truth about human sexuality. This lays the groundwork for a responsible and satisfying adult sexual adaptation. Can we undertake the same approach to teaching realistically about death? Teaching children the truth about human sexuality does not make them "sex-fiends"; nor does teaching the truth about death make people depressed.

Religions, too, can serve to deny death by making it unreal. Promises of a "better life" after death, a rebirth, or the transmigration of the soul into another body imply that death is really illusory, and can too easily dispense the soul-wrenching that leads to an acceptance of mortality. This is not to say that what religions teach about death is false. To believe that our essence is not ended by death, but rather, is in some way changed, is truly an awesome thought.

All the major religions hold teachings about death transcendence, although they differ in the nature of this transcendence and its relationship to life on earth. And a significant proportion of the world's people believe in some form of death survival. This is a viable and sustaining belief. In considering an afterlife, however, what we must first be certain of is that we die; we have had a beginning and will have an end. To live a full life we need to embrace this fact before we can find meaning in a post-death existence.

The fear of death is really the fear of nothingness. This connects to fears of abandonment, rejection, and being replaced by another. Although these fears exist independently, they are interconnected, and one often gets expressed in the other. This can be dramatically seen in children whose abandonment by nurturant others can mean death, or when children are brutalized by the simple uncaring of parents.

There is a particular type of psychological adaptation called reaction formation. This behavior pattern desensitizes a fear by directly confronting it, challenging the object of the fear to do its worst and, by surviving, "proves" the fear has no power. This type of adaptation is seen in the Don Juan character, whose fear of impotence leads to repeated sexual conquests, thereby "proving" that he is virile. Vocational choices are frequently made in response to a perceived weakness or fear: The one who fears insanity becomes a psychotherapist; one afraid of animals becomes a lion-tamer; the long-distance swimmer conquers a fear of water.

It should not surprise us, then, that the fear of death shows itself in life choices. Those who undertake daredevil stunts, who walk up to the face of death and symbolically thumb their nose at it, may have deep-seated fears around death contained by their behavior. Such activities keep fear at bay. But they also hinder our ability to cope with the fear of death in a more integrated way. For example, the physician who chooses medicine hoping to conquer death may have great difficulty when one of his or her patients dies. The patient's death serves as evidence of the inability to conquer death, and thereby exposes the physician's vulnerability.

Coming to Terms with Mortality

The destructive potential in the denial of death was dramatically shown to me by a client. My initial impression of Harry was of a robust, vigorous, somewhat overbearing man. He came to see me at the insistence of his family physician, who had been prescribing tranquilizers for Harry for some time. Although it was only a mild muscle relaxant, his dosage was fairly high and the physician had reservations about keeping him on the medication for an extended period of time.

Harry had suffered several panic attacks, a disabling condition that made it difficult for him to be effective in his position as a high school principal. The first attack, a mild one, occurred approximately three years ago at a faculty meeting. He was about to address the assemblage when he broke out in a cold sweat, feeling his throat constrict and his legs go rubbery. Harry got through the attack by firmly grasping the podium, lowering his head as if collecting his thoughts, and taking several deep breaths.

The second time it struck he was entering the auditorium for another faculty meeting. This time the panic was more severe; in addition to the sweats and rubbery legs, he could hear his heart pounding and felt a painful constriction in his chest. He was sure he was having a heart attack, and was taken to the emergency room of a local hospital. No evidence of any cardiac illness was found, but he was kept overnight for observation, and discharged the next day with no evidence of physical pathology.

The third attack came when he was about to leave his office for another staff meeting; this time it struck in full force.

Not only were the distressing physical symptoms back, but in addition, he was flooded with a terrifying conviction that he was about to die. Rushed to the hospital, he was given intravenous tranquilization, and the panic subsided. Again, extensive tests showed no physiological cause.

After that, a combination of medication and an avoidance of staff meetings kept the attacks at bay. Harry was convinced that if he stopped the medication an attack would come, thus he was willing to see me.

Treatment of panic attacks must utilize some behavioral components, or the fear of another attack will become more disabling than the attack itself. Avoidance increases the fear, which may eventually become insurmountable, much like when, as a child, you were made to get back on the bicycle after your fall. However, Harry needed to work on what lay behind his fear before he could directly confront it and go back to a faculty meeting.

Harry was 51 years old, married, with three children, the oldest a 15-year-old son. He had entered the military right from high school, doing two tours of duty in Vietnam. He did not like to talk about this experience, and the little he did say was detached from affect. After two terms of enlistment, Harry came home to go to college, and got a degree in physical education. He taught in high school and coached hockey, while getting a masters degree in educational administration. Marrying at 34, he and his wife had their children soon after.

Harry was still active athletically, rising at 5:00 am three days a week to go to the ice rink and play hockey with friends. Friday nights he went "out with the boys" at the local Elks Lodge; many of his days off were spent on his 28-foot boat with his fishing gear and a six-pack of beer. All in all, Harry was a good man, who supported his family, never cheated on his wife, went to church every Sunday (well, almost), did his job well, cared about the students in his school, and was generous with his time in community service. So why the panic attacks?

A few things about Harry were striking. First, he compartmentalized his emotions, and was cut off from his feelings. As we have seen, this often happens when there are difficult or anxiety-evoking emotions that cannot be coped with in a more direct manner. Secondly, there was a nonreflectiveness about him, in spite of his level of education. He went through all the motions of life without stopping to reflect on what it all really meant. For instance, he went to church regularly but it seemed to be something he just did, without the experience touching him in some transformative way. When I asked him what would be different if he was not a church member, he said, not entirely jocosely, that "it would leave Sunday mornings free for hockey."

The third clue to Harry's panic attacks was in his choice of activities outside of work. He was a vigorous man with a great deal of energy, but this energy seemed devoted to holding onto the past. His hockey playing, beer drinking, and desire to be "one of the guys"—none of which is bad or wrong in itself—coalesced into a picture of a 51-year-old man trying to be 21 years old.

When I asked what being 51 meant to him, he pursed his lips and said, "I don't think of myself as 51... That's getting old, and I don't feel old. I can retire at 55, but what would I do? You know, my father died when he was 53!" These were hardly disconnected thoughts. Let us look at them thematically to understand what they said: denial ("I don't think/feel old"), nothingness ("what would I do?"—read "be") and death ("my father died when...").

An additional factor in this man's life was the fact that his oldest son was now an adolescent. A life crisis is often precipitated when a same-sex child reaches this stage. The child is at the beginning of sexual potency, in the spring of adulthood with all its experiences lying before him or her. Concurrently, the parent may feel that his or her potency is waning. Harry was also approaching the age at which his father died. He consciously denied any fear of death, quoting Woody Allen: "I'm not afraid of death, I just don't want to be there when it happens." This statement revealed more fear than he cared to admit.

During therapy, Harry reported a recurrent dream which gave more direct access to his fear. In the dream, he was back in the army, in a room full of soldiers from his old outfit. Harry was aware of being a civilian, although he was in full-dress uniform, standing apart from a group of soldiers who were discussing something. He was unable to speak or move, and stood passively while the other soldiers talked, totally ignoring him. During the dream, Harry was aware of having left his job and family to rejoin the army. Everything he had achieved to that point was gone, and he awoke feeling anxious.

Harry often had this dream, with slight variations. Without going into too much detail, I believe the dream was about death. His military experience was a major part of his young adulthood. Although he claimed he did not like army life, he had enlisted twice; the army gave him both an identity and a sense of belonging. In his dream, however, he was no longer an active part of the picture. He had lost his place, his speech, and his power; everything he had achieved, both in the military and in his life afterward, was gone. He was like the corpse at a wake service.

In therapy, we used the dream to bring his anxiety to the

surface. Here he was able to confront his own mortality and fear of death, and accept it in a more realistic and integrative way. He also saw how his "youth-seeking" behavior kept a conscious awareness of death at a distance.

Harry began to open up about his Vietnam experiences and the deaths of his comrades. He was able to see how the background of his dream—losing all he had achieved since leaving the military, to become a soldier again—was an attempt to cope with the guilt he felt about having survived when so many did not. By sacrificing his achievements and going back to being a soldier, Harry used atonement and retribution in his dream to assuage his unconscious guilt.

Why did Harry panic around faculty meetings? Panic attacks occur in situations where one's vulnerability is in danger of being exposed. In faculty meetings, he had to "face" the faculty; they could "see" his weakness and helplessness in the face of guilt, aging, and death. The attacks were triggered now, and not earlier in his life, because he was close to his father's age of death, at the same time dealing with his son's emerging adolescence.

Harry used the insights gained through therapy to change his behavior. He recognized that he was not going to enjoy the afternoon of his life if he kept wishing it were the morning. When he faced his fear of death and of the nothingness it would bring, he could then understand what his religion taught about life and death, and open his heart to its meaning. No miraculous conversion occurred, only a gentle acceptance of how vulnerable he felt as he owned his mortality. For Harry, being alive now took on a new sweetness.

The time came for him to go back to those dreaded faculty meetings. I agreed to attend them with him, sitting unobtrusively in the back but available, just in case. At the first meeting he simply attended, and let his vice-principal run the proceedings. The next time, Harry opened the meeting with a brief statement, then turned the agenda over to the vice-principal. He expanded his role at subsequent meetings until he was able to chair them without any experience of panic.

It has been several years since Harry was in therapy, and he has had no return of the panic attacks. He decided not to retire at 55 and, in his last letter to me, was considering applying for an associate superintendent's position. He had become a lay minister in his church, visiting the aged and infirm as part of his ministry. He also gave up hockey, and became an avid tennis player. As a P.S. to his letter, Harry wrote that he never again had the dream about finding himself back in the army.

Harry needed to fully embrace the reality of his own mortality and all that death signified for him if he was to live as fully as he could within the life he had. To a significant degree, his fear of death was killing him by robbing him of the pleasure of simply being alive. It is only in fully embracing the fact of our death, and that of all those whose presence we cherish, that we can fully experience all this life has to offer.

Questions for Discussion

1. What are your beliefs, religious or philosophical, about the place of death in the scheme of life? What do you fear the most about your own death? What are your hopes about death? If possible, share your fears and hopes related to death with another person.

2. What myths about death do you relate to? Do these myths help you to accept death, or are they a way of avoiding its reality?

3. "We need to fully embrace our own mortality if we are to live life in the fullest way." In the light of what you have read in this chapter, what does this statement mean to you?

4. As teachers, parents, and responsible adults, how do we teach children about death in a way that is truthful and honest? How can we help them integrate the reality of death with life, in a way that does not cripple or overwhelm them with anxiety?

CHAPTER 11

FREEDOM

The second eternal truth is that we have the absolute freedom to create our life from the choices we make. Most of us think of freedom as an unmixed blessing, something that we would wage war to keep. If anyone, be it government or individual, tries to take away our freedom, we resist their attempts to interfere with our rights, and may even do the opposite of what is asked just to flaunt our freedom.

Yet do we really want to be free? Do we focus on resisting overt constraints on freedom while willingly surrendering to covert ones? Perhaps we surrender because we really do not want freedom and give it up with a sigh of relief, as long as we can maintain the illusion of personal freedom. We are actually terrified of fully embracing our freedom, and exercising it in those areas of our life where it really counts.

To be free means to assume responsibility for ourselves. Without this assumption freedom is meaningless, nothing more than an exercise in irresponsibility. To be responsible means that we create our own life, build our own path within the realities that God or nature hands to us. This is an awesome task, and the cause of great existential anxiety.

Jean-Paul Sartre defines personal freedom and its attendant responsibility as "being the authors of our own lives." Each of us writes the drama that is our life, unquestionably limited by the materials we have to write with, but nonetheless, creating the script for our existence. This is a heavy burden. It is much easier to bemoan our fate and blame others for our deficits, defeats, and travails, rather than accept what we have and build the life we choose. Yet we must author our own destiny, and be responsible for what we do with the failures and frustrations that inevitably occur.

Too many of us would give our freedom over to powerful institutions in return for being fed, housed, clothed, and kept free from victimization. This is not to say that governments do not have a responsibility to assist those who are unable to maintain a decent lifestyle, or provide collective protection when individuals cannot protect themselves. Governments should be judged by how well they care for their weakest members; of necessity, we sacrifice some freedom to sustain the collective so it can act on our behalf when we are unable to as individuals.

But each time government moves to make our lives more safe or secure, it enacts the price of a piece of our freedom. Witness the drop in crime in North America; although there may be less crime this year than a decade ago, we are also living day-to-day with being less free than we were a decade ago. To be totally crime-free has a price, and the bill is in sacrifice of freedoms. In spite of this we still retain the responsibility, and the freedom, to create our life, even though this freedom is reduced by conditions within which we live. The ultimate responsibility is always ours.

The most difficult task any therapist faces is to enable a client to assume responsibility for himself or herself. We would all like someone to solve our problems, give us a recipe or formula to make everything all right. We all want to be told "how to do it," and given the panacea that would make us happy. Yet there are no readily available answers or solutions to complex human struggles, no recipes, formulae, or rules for happiness. Only the paths we create for ourselves lead to a happy life. Others, like a therapist, can walk along and be eyes for what we are not seeing, or ears for what we are not hearing. But we must then take action on what we learn from therapy or from our relations with others, and the choice of what course to take is ours alone.

To be free means to make choices, to make decisions without an infallible view of the future. This can be terrifying, because once we act on our choice, we lose the opportunity to select alternatives. We may make the "wrong" choice, and be stuck; other options may no longer be available.

To ease the burden of this responsibility people often give up their freedom by giving themselves over to a person, cause, or institution. The abandonment of freedom, however, is so stultifying and growth-inhibiting that a feeling of oppression inevitably arises, and forces a demand for freedom. This pattern occurs in governments and institutions over and over again; no matter how benevolent the oppressor, the instinct toward freedom always reasserts itself and fuels rebellion.

The real human struggle is not the conflict between oppressive institutions and freedom for those oppressed, as significant as this struggle is. Rather, the struggle lies in our willingness to give away our freedom in order to be relieved of its burden. The relief from relinquishing our freedom is illusory; the burden remains, and we are condemned to our absolute freedom. Even the gods will not take it back. We are caught between being terrified of freedom and the inability to give it up.

The fear of freedom can be so overwhelming that many feel helpless and powerless in the face of choice. Out of this sense of impotence we may reach for an omnipotent Being, whose will can guide us in our choices. We surrender our freedom to God; our sole responsibility, then, is to do the will of God. The Muslim's submission to the will of Allah is an acknowledgment of determinism; the only freedom is to accept or not accept. A Christian's endeavor to discover the will of God and conform to it is often an abdication of responsibility done in the name of divine will.

I do not question the possibility of a divine will or plan operative in the universe. This is an awesome thought, and deserves to be pondered. But is it possible that we give up responsibility for our lives by assigning our freedom to God's will? If so, this evasion keeps us from fully experiencing our own existence. The divine plan—both on an individual and global basis—is realized only when we accept our individual freedom, and exercise our choices in a manner that expresses a moral and God-like integrity. Then, we may come to see that we are carrying out some role in a transcendent drama, that there is a synchronicity to life's events which our decisions either facilitate or hinder.

It is not my intention to challenge any religious doctrine of divine providence. I do, however, challenge the way some people use doctrine as an evasion of freedom. Each of us has to eventually surrender to our own vulnerability, our help-lessness in the face of life forces beyond our control, finding strength in this surrender and power in our vulnerability. But we freely choose this surrender and accept its reality, assuming responsibility for our decision as well as for the other ones that have shaped us.

Those who reach this stage in spirituality often find themselves moving away from a sense of "God's will," seeing their task more in making decisions and accepting the consequences. The goal of life, then, becomes more what self we create, rather than counting our achievements or accumulating acts of charity. Living is an ongoing act of self-creation through the choices made within the circumstances given us. Who we are at the ending of our lives is the only significant monument to our existence.

Making Choices, Taking Risks

Anne, a 27-year-old woman, vibrant, intelligent, and attractive, sat facing me. From all outward appearances, she was highly successful, facing an enviable decision—but paralyzed in her ability to make that choice. Three years out of law school with a specialty in tax law, she was employed by a prestigious Eastern law firm. She had recently been offered a promotion which would lead to an eventual partnership. However, she could not decide whether to accept or reject the offer.

Anne repeatedly weighed the pros and cons of each course of action, trying to separate her thoughts from her feelings about the promotion. If she delayed much longer, a decision would be made for her, a situation she clearly wanted to avoid. Yet she could not bring herself to make a decision on her own.

From my perspective, the decision was obvious: Take the

promotion. The move offered more money, little dislocation in her personal life, and great opportunities for the future. Along with the increased responsibility, Anne's career would take an even greater priority in her life than it currently had; but nothing else I could see would weigh against her acceptance of the firm's offer. Since the decision had to come from her, however, I needed to understand her life if I was to help in any way with her decision.

Anne was raised in a typical middle-class Boston family, the only girl in a family of three children. Her mother was an outgoing woman and the dominating force in the family, a homemaker who returned to work when her daughter was a high school junior. Anne's father was a second generation American who grew up in relative poverty. A veteran of World War II, he went to college on the G.I. Bill, joined the tax department of a banking firm after graduation, and worked his way up to the inner circle of the bank's management.

Both parents were noted for their strong, rather conservative and racially tinged opinions on political and social issues; Senator Joseph McCarthy was their hero. Anne's own beliefs were quite at odds with those of her parents, but she shared none of her opinions at home for the sake of keeping peace.

Early in life Anne was recognized as brighter than either of her brothers, and was seen as special because of this. She could have done well in school without effort, but this was not her style; she worked hard at everything she did. Her parents sacrificed to send her to a private high school, and supported her through one of the Seven Sisters colleges, as well as through the best law school in Boston. Her parents not only took great pride in her, but invested her with great trust, simply expecting her to always do what was right. Anne never disappointed them.

She started dating in her third year of high school and had a series of boyfriends through college and law school. None of the boys she dated was the type her parents might object to. Anne thought she would like the security and comfort of marriage, but was willing to wait until she met someone to whom she really wanted to commit. Although she noticed that the pool of available men was dwindling, she had a full enough life for now and was confident that at some point she would marry and have a family.

Anne gave no evidence of depression or undue anxiety, and seemed free of all other psychological symptoms. Then why was she unable to make a decision about her career? Why was she so paralyzed when most people would have leapt at the opportunity offered her? Obviously, some conflict kept her from taking the risk inherent in every decision. Her fear had her paralyzed, but it was a fear that she was not aware of.

In our time together, we discovered that Anne had made very few decisions in life that were actually hers. On the surface, the decisions all seemed like hers; no one ever told her explicitly what to do. But every choice—from the schools she attended, to the boys she dated, the friends she made, and the career she followed—was based on her knowledge of what would please her parents. Anne was now at a point, however, where her parents' desires could no longer motivate her own decisions.

Additionally, accepting the promotion would mean that she would disappoint her parents in a fundamental way, so subtle that neither she nor her parents could articulate it. Anne's parents were both in late middle age, a stage of life where one becomes actively aware of the possibility—and expectation—of being a grandparent. This development opens up an avenue of growth which gives us a new image and sense of personal significance as our parenting and career roles wane. Grandchildren also provide us with a reassuring glimpse that our genes and our name will carry into the future. And because grandparents have such a vital role to play in the psychological development of their grandchildren, nature prepares for this by placing that generative impulse inside all of us. As we feel a sense of incompleteness if we fail to parent, there is a similar feeling of incompleteness if we fail to grandparent.

This was the situation that Anne's parents found themselves in, and it was on Anne, rather than on her brothers, that they placed their hopes for grandparenting. Of course, this was never actually verbalized; but the empathetic bond was such that there was no way that Anne could not be aware of this expectation, albeit unconsciously. Thus her dilemma: If she decided to accept the promotion, it would move her further away from getting married and starting a family.

Anne was happy with her life, and she was living it the way she wanted to. Until the promotion was offered to her, this ran along the same path as what her parents wanted for her. Because she had been so successful in her life choices, Anne believed that as long as she did what they wanted, she could not fail. Now, however, she was strongly tempted to diverge from the safe path of parental expectations. Could she do this? Was following her parents' will the talisman that brought success, and would she court disaster if she left it behind?

Anne was being called to make a serious life choice, yet she was terrified that she might decide wrong, and fail. In therapy, we could discuss why she was having so much difficulty making a decision; but ultimately, she had to take action, and assume responsibility for making a choice.

Anne was unable to make a decision. Torn between doing what she needed to do for herself so that her life bore fruit and meeting parental expectations, she could not respond and the offer was withdrawn. Subsequently, she was able to positively incorporate the anger she felt for her life sacrifices; this anger became a core strength in her character.

About 18 months later another offer came, this one in a Western city with a newly formed law firm, and with the potential and the capital for growth. She accepted this offer, moved away from her parents, and made a life for herself that is deeply satisfying. Incidentally, she met someone there, albeit from a rival law firm, and they have married. She phoned me just a few months ago, not just to update me on her life, but to let me know that she was pregnant, an event she welcomed for its own sake.

Her situation was a lot like skydiving: You stand at the door of the plane, and summon up the courage to make the dive. Everyone can tell you what a thrill it is to fly off into space, but at some point you have to close your eyes, grit your teeth and, all by yourself, leap. This is essentially the burden that freedom imposes on us.

Questions for Discussion

1. To be truly free is live in the awareness that you can make yourself into the person you choose to be, in spite of the efforts of individuals or institutions to oppress you. How have you evaded this truth by becoming what "they" want for the sake of something "they" were able to give you? What price have you paid to live in fidelity to the person you are?

2. What did you learn about responsibility and choices from this chapter? What steps do you need to take to become

fully responsible for your choices? How do you deal with the failures and frustrations that choices sometimes bring?

3. What in your upbringing has allowed you to fully embrace responsibility and freedom? Have your religious beliefs helped or hindered you in becoming the author of your life? What doctrines or maxims do you blindly accept that prevent a full embrace of freedom?

CHAPTER 12

ALONENESS

The third eternal truth is that ultimately, we are alone. We are born alone and die alone; in between, there is a part of each of us essentially isolated from all others, a place inside that no other person is able to touch. No matter how hard we try to make ourselves known, there will always be some part of us that no one will be able to understand, an impregnable solitude where we are totally alone. This is the existential anxiety of aloneness.

Within the state of aloneness, there are three kinds of isolation. First is an *interpersonal* isolation, when we lack friends or intimate relationships with others. We can relieve this situation by taking steps to have friendships and intimacies in our life. This includes joining social groups, going places where people gather, taking part in community events and activities, and taking an interest in what interests others. We can even put a personal ad in the paper. If all these attempts fail, then we might look inward to address what may sabotage our efforts at relating to others.

A second condition is *intrapersonal* isolation, where we are strangers to ourselves. This frequently comes about when we do not understand ourselves, reject who and what we are, or disown pieces of ourselves, be they positive or negative. Here we live under false pretenses, sliding into inauthenticity. The usual symptom of this situation is depression. We can do something about this by making an effort to live in more authentic ways, through self-owning and self-acceptance. Whenever we strive to live in our own truth we eliminate intrapersonal isolation.

The third type of isolation is *existential*; this we can do nothing about, other than accept it. This is the essential isolation that each of us experiences in moments of quiet, solitude, crisis, pain, defeat, depression, grief, or other intensely emotional times. This isolation reaches into the deepest recesses of our being, and forces us to be aware that we stand alone in life.

That there is an uncrossable gulf between ourselves and others is fact; how we cope with it affects our life experience. Many of us try to deny it through a variety of maneuvers, most of which involve attaching ourselves to another to avoid experiencing this aloneness. Life then becomes an unsatisfying, desperate search for that special person with whom we can achieve perfect unity, thereby vitiating all sense of aloneness. The only time in our lives that we are completely "at one" with another, where all our needs are totally met, is in our mother's womb. Here there is absolute safety and security. But there is no way we can ever go back to the womb.

Others of us avoid being alone at all, finding it discomforting to not have someone around. Aloneness drives us to leave our room, apartment, or house to be with others: Any solitude is intolerable. If we must be alone, the radio or TV is on, providing some reassurance from the sound of voices. We need to feel a continuous connectedness with others. The fear of facing our inner solitude is too great.

Some people enter marriage expecting a partner exclusively devoted to them, who will meet all their needs, with whom they can live in blissful paradise. But the only person in our lives who will ever be totally dedicated to us is our mother or father, and this parenting relationship has to end in order for us to become mature adults. Marriage, then, can be a rude awakening when we discover that no one can replace our mother or father. We must give up this expectation in order to share our reality with another person who has needs, desires, expectations, and demands of their own.

Part of the myth of romance is the search for the one person who can cure us of our aloneness and isolation. In North American society, we glorify this romantic conception of love, and promote the illusion. Our idyllic sense of "falling in love," wherein we become totally absorbed in the loved one, and he or she totally involved in us, blunts the painful reality of the wall of separation that surrounds each of us.

For several years, I was the therapist for a Roman Catholic priest named Paul. In many ways, this man was a fine minister who provided excellent spiritual leadership to the parishes he had pastored over the years. But he had come to realize that he had deep conflicts in his life, and sought psychotherapy.

Paul had a certain charisma that drew others to him, men as well as women. Men liked his rugged masculinity, his ability to be "one of the guys." With women he showed a different self, a more vulnerable side, talking about loneliness, feelings of inadequacy, fears of failure, and other things he never discussed with male friends. He was a masculine buddy to men, and a vulnerable little boy to women. Both images were unconsciously intended to seduce others into giving him narcissistic gratification and the reassuring affirmation of acceptance.

Although voluntarily committed to celibacy, Paul had had numerous romantic involvements with women over the 22 years since his ordination. The pattern of his involvement was remarkably similar in each case. It would begin innocently enough with a secretary, a parishioner seeking counsel, a co-member on some committee, or a simple chance encounter. The relationship would then move quickly from a professional to a personal one; he and the women would "fall in love," and show it with increasing expressions of intimacy.

While these relationships were highly erotic, they never culminated in sexual intercourse. Paul wanted only to receive love, not give it. He would, however, become highly infatuated with the woman, thinking about her all the time, devising ways to be together, wanting to run away and live in bliss-filled happiness forever. He told each woman of his love for her. Each woman responded in kind, then would inevitably ask, "What about the future?"

At this point, the relationship would fall apart. He would consciously struggle with his dilemma: Should he give up the priesthood for this woman, choose her over God? In each case, he could not reconcile his own weakness for the woman with the call to priesthood, and gave up the relationship for the sake of his ministry. In tear-filled agony, he would tell the woman he could never see her again.

Paul would then go to his bishop and, with pain-laced contrition, confess all. The bishop understood how men were tempted and how passions could overwhelm. What was important was that the priest mend his ways, recommit to a celibate priesthood, and be transferred to a distant parish where he could not be found by the abandoned lover. This was done, and within a short time there would be another innocent flirtation, then involvement, subsequent bout of guilt and recommitment, another termination of the relationship, and a fresh start for Paul.

The Further Implications

It is obvious that there are ethical and legal issues here, in addition to moral ones; there are questions around the violation of the priest's professional responsibilities, the exploitation of the women, and the irresponsibility of disregarding those who were his victims. The bishop also bears responsibility for colluding with and perhaps encouraging this man's abusive behaviors. But this is not my concern here. Although all of us bear a responsibility toward the eradication of abusive behavior, the psychotherapist's role is to treat the abuser, and thereby address whatever psychological factors contribute to such behavior.

Several dynamics could have motivated the compulsive heterosexuality of this priest: fear of impotency, the reassurance that a woman would respond to him, fears of homosexuality, the need for excitement to ward off underlying depression, an unconscious hostility for women, leading to the hurtful behavior of seduction and abandonment, or the desire to affirm his adulthood and masculine power through achieving a conquest. It was also possible that he sought a way out of the priesthood but, being unable to make that decision, hoped circumstances might force the choice. Although any one of these was a plausible explanation, none seemed operative with this priest.

Paul's life story provided the explanation for his behavior. His parents were high school sweethearts who married just before his father went off to serve in World War II. His father had been a high school athlete, wholesome and popular, the ideal young man in 1940s America. His mother loved the father all through high school; all her ambitions and fantasies for the future included him. Life was full of promise on the August day in 1942 when they wed.

The father returned from the war in early 1945, a genuine hero who had won a Silver Star, but missing a leg and totally deaf. The celebratory adulation upon his return quickly faded, and he soon became just another crippled laborer, struggling to support his family on meager wages supplemented by government disability checks. The dreams that Paul's parents had shared when they first married, so full of colorful promise, blended into the dull grayness of post-war reality. The father was now filled with anger at the dreariness of his life, while the mother became a bitter, withdrawn martyr, burdened by being a wife and mother.

Paul was the second of his parents' two children, born three years after his brother, Bob. The boys grew up in marked contrast to each other, with the older constantly in trouble. Throughout Bob's school years his parents made countless visits to the teachers and principal to discuss his behavior. He was often truant, got a girl pregnant while both were in high school, and had numerous scrapes with the police. Alcohol abuse was a problem by the time he was a junior in high school. Shortly after graduation, Bob was arrested for breaking into a home. While on probation for that offense, he was arrested for armed assault and sent to prison. Since then, he had been in and out of jail, an antisocial, alcoholic misfit.

Paul was just the opposite. He did well in school, was a good athlete, and became very popular with his classmates. In fact, most of the townspeople compared him to the way his father was in high school, especially regarding the good looks and charm of both. Paul's decision to enter the seminary after high school was no surprise, since everyone saw him as someone who would make an ideal priest.

Invariably, the comparison was made between Paul and his brother: how different they both were! In reality, however, they were not very different at all. Both were angry, hurting men, struggling to make a connection to parents who were emotionally frozen. One brother became "bad," and the other "good." Yet each was screaming out to be recognized, acknowledged, and loved, to be helped to feel that he was not alone in the universe. Bob gave vent to his rage, and bottled up his need for tenderness; Paul vented his need for tenderness, bottling up his rage.

As an adult, Paul desperately sought the affirmation that comes from being loved by a woman. He wanted a woman to become totally immersed in him, to know that he was the most important person to her and that she would give up everything for him. Being loved would assuage his deep sense of isolation. But he could never commit to love, because he knew how much it hurt to lose love. He was addicted to falling in love, and went from relationship to relationship, coming close in each to the point of commitment, then moving on. He could never let himself grow in love or even just be in love.

When we attempt to fuse with another person we try to eradicate the anxiety that our essential isolation creates in us. If we become infatuated with someone, there is fusion taking place, albeit on a superficial level. One is totally involved with the other; he thinks only of her, she wants to be with him alone. Nothing matters except togetherness, and for the moment, all life's problems fade away. We gravitate to this place because it wipes away the source of our fear, our con-demnation to aloneness, even if only temporarily.

Infatuation is a valid stage in learning to love another. It is not until infatuation fades, however, that we begin to under-stand what it really means to love another. This is the differ-ence between "falling in love" and "being in love." Invariably, infatuation dies, and it may or may not leave love in its wake. Inevitably, the object of our infatuation will come to disap-point us, because no one can assuage the essential aloneness that exists in the heart of each of us. Our choice is to struggle with this aloneness or embrace it as a human reality, with the greater profit in the latter choice.

Religions teach that God is present in every moment of our life, and that this God knows us in the deepest reaches of our being. God is aware of all our thoughts, wishes, and desires, and understands our pain, disappointment, and suffering even better than we do. Nothing about us is hidden from God. If God's eternal presence is not enough for us, there are guardian angels, the spirits of the deceased, and intercessory saints who also walk with us and protect us through life. Never being alone, we need never feel alone.

These thoughts and beliefs can be the source of great conso-lation in moments of isolation. But if we accept religious doctrine in order to avoid our essential aloneness, we risk stunting our spirituality. Becoming aware of our solitariness creates the space that permits a surrender to God. Here all becomes one, a unity that breaks the barrier of human separateness. In embracing our aloneness we discover the way to transcend it.

In the same way that we cannot use God or religious doc-trine, another person will not ward off the pain of our inner aloneness. Because there is no "cure" for this type of isolation, no one can permanently take it away, in spite of temporary respites from our conscious awareness of it. Therefore, relationships undertaken to avoid existential aloneness will eventually collapse, and hinder the nurturing companionship available to us with friendships and intimacies.

To surrender to loving another means taking the risk of investing all we have, with no holding back, into the hands of another. It also means that we permit ourselves to be loved by the other, and try to respond to their love with our own. We will still own our separateness, since two can never fully become one. But our loneliness becomes more bearable knowing that we have a companion to walk with, a soul mate with whom we feel known and accepted.

Questions for Discussion

1. When do you feel most acutely that inner isolation, the unbridgeable gap between yourself and others? Is this a comfortable feeling, a place you like to go into from time to time? Or is it a discomforting place that you rush to escape from? How can you feel more at peace with your ultimate aloneness?

2. What unrealistic expectations do you have for the person with whom you are most intimate? (Perhaps you can discover what these are by looking at how that person disappoints you.) With what realistic expectations can you replace the unrealistic ones?

3. Do your religious beliefs anesthetize you to your ultimate aloneness, or do they make you more sensitive to it? Have you really examined the beliefs that you use to cope with your fear of isolation so that they are yours, rather than something you have unreflectively accepted?

CHAPTER 13

MEANINGLESSNESS

The fourth, and last, eternal truth is the possibility that life is meaningless. It can be overwhelming to realize that our life may have no more transcendent meaning than the life of any other animate or inanimate being. We know that we are born, reproduce, live a number of years, and die, just like all the other animals. Each human has a single lifespan, one solitary precious life.

Yet, to make meaning out of our experience is instinctual to humans. Our eyes see shapes and colors, our ears make sounds out of vibrations, our mouth and nose turn chemicals into tastes and smells, while our skin changes pressure and temperature into touch and warmth. We see people, hear birds sing, taste chocolate, smell roses, feel the warmth of a spring day and the cool breeze of evening.

In fact, we cannot *not* make meaning of the input of our senses; this configuring of electrochemical reactions into meaningful experiences happens automatically. Whenever our senses get stimulated, our mind/body goes on alert, becoming curious and wary, looking to discover what the sound, smell, taste, touch, or movement is all about. Our brain takes data from our senses, interprets it, and tells us what we should do.

But where is it written that life itself has meaning? Spirituality demands that before we can really discover a transformative meaning to life, we must confront meaninglessness. We must be open to the possibility that life has no meaning, and all is in vain. Perhaps this is the issue faced by Jesus in the garden of Gethsemene, or Socrates as he held the hemlock, or countless martyrs as they fell victim to the brutality of other humans.

In a previous chapter, I wrote that the primary spiritual task is to find a philosophy of life that gives meaning and purpose to existence. But suppose there really is no meaning or purpose? This immediately brings into question all our moral values, because *how* we live is contingent on *why* we live; the values we live by are dependent on what purpose we see in our existence. If it has none, then values are simply social conventions that make living in proximity to each other easier and safer. They are both relative and pragmatic.

It is not easy to accept the possibility of meaninglessness. We grasp at anything that will say it is not so, that life does have meaning and purpose. All religions provide a transcendent value to existence, and we hold onto these beliefs with passion. People are willing to give up life itself to preserve a belief in the transcendent; witness martyrs to the faith or to a political cause. To become a martyr is the noblest of acts; we erect monuments to honor those who died for a cause, and name our children after those who died for faith.

Several decades ago, I stood with a group of foreign visitors in a cemetery just outside the city of Leningrad in Russia. Our tour guide spoke to us of the siege of Leningrad by the Nazis, recalling the thousands upon thousands of people who died in that conflict, and were buried in the mass graves stretching out before us.

She spoke of a Russian soldier, who had first served under the Tsar, then came over to the side of the Bolsheviks and became a general in the People's Army. This general was captured by the Nazis early in World War II, and, because of his great military skill, was offered a commission in the German Army in exchange for his life. He refused.

Sentenced to die, the general was stripped of his clothes, and forced to march a mile to the town square, naked, on a freezing February morning. There he was sprayed with water, in a mist that iced on contact, until he became a solid block of ice. His body remained frozen in the town square, until the townspeople buried him with the spring thaw.

As the tour guide recounted the tale, she made no effort to hide her tears. Although the woman had been only a child when this event took place, her grief was sincere and heartfelt. The general was a martyr to the cause of the Russian people, an honored hero and genuine saint. I was reminded of the stories I had heard as a child in Sunday school, of the Christian martyrs who went to their deaths rather than compromise their beliefs. These stories were told by our teachers with the same reverential conviction as this Russian woman told hers.

The germination of faith is inherent in the question "Why?" Early in life we are taught about God, and that we are punished for sin and rewarded for virtue. We are instructed to live responsibly, fulfill our obligations, and strive for excellence. These teachings presuppose that life has some meaning beyond itself; yet what if it does not?

Each of us needs to wrestle with the question, "What meaning does my life have?" If we have previously accepted an answer passed on to us by cultural heritage or religious tradition, then we should reexamine the answer. In light of our life experiences and learned knowledge, do any of the traditional answers to life's meaning hold true? We must become open to the possibility that life has no absolute meaning if an answer is to become spiritually transformative for us.

Our ability to cope with the other three eternal truths—death, freedom, and aloneness—depends on our belief about the meaning of life. If life has a meaning, then the three are at least tolerable, possibly even acceptable. If life has no meaning, then the premise for understanding and fashioning a response to the first three truths becomes negated. Thus, whatever meaning there is to life must be discovered, and arise, out of our own search.

There are several nonspiritual—or anti-spiritual—ways to escape a sense of life's meaninglessness. Each holds out the promise of escaping aloneness, achieving immortality, and, above all, avoidance of the terror of a meaningless existence. These nonspiritual means help people resolve existential dilemmas and provide a reason for living; yet they constrict, rather than expand, our spirit. The three ways most commonly used are affluence, power, and sex.

If only we were affluent, and had enough money, we would feel at ease, never anxious, totally secure. Life would be idyllic. We could do what we want, when we want, and be beholden to no one. Every day would be full and exciting, with nothing to fear. Yet if, by chance, we reached a point where we had more money than we could ever spend, we would discover that our aloneness still gnaws, death still stares us in the face, and we still question the meaninglessness of the life we have created for ourselves. Affluence does not make us happy; the evidence of this is overwhelming. Being rich and miserable may be better than being poor and miserable, but the misery is just as real. Wealth does not erase the life issues that are part of all of us.

Power also holds out the promise of an escape from life's anxieties. If we have power, people flock to us. We are free to do whatever we want, and will live forever in the monuments that we have created with our power. Power gives control, and if we are in control we can structure reality exactly as we want it. But this, too, is not a solution; misery will sleep with those who exercise power as comfortably as it will with the victims of oppression.

Why is sex such a powerful draw on the human personality? We have made sex into a business that probably is larger than AT&T, General Motors, Sony, and Toyota combined. We spend a great deal of time thinking about sex, buy books and magazines that describe it to us, pay for films that show others "doing it," and commit a major portion of our energy to its pursuit. Why are we the only animal that pursues sex, along with affluence and power, as an end in itself?

We are obsessed with sex because, like money and power, it anesthetizes us to our deeper anxieties. Pornography may serve as a source of erotic stimulation, but that fact alone would not have turned it into a multibillion-dollar industry. Sex promises a respite from aloneness, a place where we can totally merge with another and overcome our essential isolation. It further propels us into the romantic notion that, in achieving union with another, we can live for, and in, the other, while the other does the same for us. Making each other happy becomes our reason for existence, thus overcoming the meaninglessness of life. Even death loses its ugliness, because we will always live in the heart of another, united in death as in life.

The advertising industry understands the meaning sex holds for us. Sex appears to remove boredom, fill our days and nights with excitement, provide us with constant companionship, release us from the burden of responsibility, and make us eternally young. All we need do is "Buy this car!" "Drink this beer..." "Wear these clothes..." or "Use this deodorant!" Although sex may be the envelope, the letter inside is about overcoming aloneness, death, responsibility, and meaning. Advertising promises a self-transcendence that is quick, easy, and undemanding.

Many people have come to understand that the false promises of popular culture can never be fulfilled. Presently, there is a renewed search for our spiritual roots, for a motivation and meaning to life that is more genuine and authentic than what has been held out in the recent past. Those coming into adulthood today see where spirituality is destroyed, where it cannot be found. They realize that the "false gods" of affluence, power, and sex cannot help us in our struggle with the existential truths. The question remains, "Where to seek?" but we now recognize many of the places we should not look.

A Compulsion for Perfection

I had barely arrived at the office one cold, blustery morning, when the phone began ringing with a demanding urgency. I rushed to pick it up, and an unusual drama commenced.

The caller was the Mother Superior to an order of medical mission sisters who worked in the poor and desperate areas of the world. This was a remarkable group of women—nurses, physicians, psychotherapists, and other health care practitioners—who gave themselves selflessly to those suffering from an oppressive poverty. I had known several of these women, and admired them for their self-transcendent commitment.

The Mother Superior apologized for her early morning call, but said she had a matter of some urgency to discuss with me. Since she would be at the Toronto airport on a brief stopover that evening, could we meet? Knowing the character and depth of this woman's life work gave me a measure of the seriousness of her request, and I readily agreed.

My curiosity was piqued by this invitation, my mind returning to it often during the day; I was in a state of high anticipation when we finally met that evening. We sat in the waiting area of the airport, as she told me of her reason for this meeting. One of her sisters, Theresa, a nurse practitioner at one of their hospitals in Central America, was in serious difficulty.

At the Central American hospital where Theresa worked, one of the hospital supervisors, in preparing for an impending government visit, made an inventory of hospital supplies and medications. The supervisor found large discrepancies between items purchased and those that were used or dispensed. Of great concern were the many prescribed medicines that were simply missing.

The hospital's internal investigation team traced the drugs to Sister Theresa. Since the amount missing was well beyond anyone's personal usage, they searched both Theresa's dispensary as well as her convent room. There the team found massive amounts of hospital supplies and drugs. Bed linens, syringes, bandages, bedpans, walkers, and more filled closets and storerooms with a supply that would have lasted over ten years in regular hospital usage.

Cases upon cases of medications were piled in the closets, many with expired usage dates. In a country where medical supplies were scarce to nonexistent, this unused hoarded supply was described by one investigator as criminal.

When confronted by her supervisor, Sister Theresa became angry and defensive. She denied using any of the medication herself, but said that it was all for her patients; she needed backup in case the government shut off the hospital from its suppliers. But, even if that happened, it would take decades for her to use what she had hoarded; most of the medications would be outdated by that time, as well, stale and useless.

The supervisor pointed out that there was no current threat of loss of drugs or supplies, and that what she was doing was illegal, poor medical practice, and threatened the very existence of the hospital. (In fact, the government of that particular country had been looking for an excuse to shunt the Sisters out of the country, suspecting them of subversive activities.) Sister Theresa would hear none of this. She became increasingly angry over not feeling understood and, when the supervisor removed her from her position, withdrew into a rage-filled, noncommunicative state.

It was decided to remove Theresa from the area to protect the integrity of the hospital, but her order was unsure what to do with her. The Motherhouse was in Rome, but there was nothing for her to do there; she would simply vegetate. The Mother Superior was convinced, rightly so as it turned out, that Sister Theresa had severe psychological issues needing immediate attention. She asked if we would take her for treatment, even though Theresa was loath to acknowledge that she had any need for psychotherapy. Although she had to come voluntarily, I agreed to do whatever we could to be of help to Sister Theresa.

I met Theresa two weeks later. A small, slightly built woman in her middle fifties, her frail appearance stood in marked contrast to the strength evident in her voice and the determined look in her eyes. She spoke precisely in English thickened by a German accent. She was quite angry about being "made to come here," and had obeyed her Superior's request only out of her vow of obedience.

Theresa felt misjudged and mistreated by the Sisters back in Central America. She insisted that she had done nothing wrong by hoarding hospital supplies and medications, being convinced that she needed them for her patients. Additionally, she was very angry over the humiliation of having been removed peremptorily from her position.

Two conditions were evident from the start. Besides her obvious surface anger, Theresa was a person who was profoundly depressed. Actually, this had been noted by a physician whom she saw while in Central America. She had gone to him with a physical complaint, for which he prescribed an antidepressant. Theresa refused to take the medication, saying that she did not feel depressed. Yet all the symptoms were present.

Theresa's life consisted entirely of work, although her energy level was so low she had to push herself to get through the day. Accompanying this fatigue was a chronic irritability. Her sleep was disturbed by early morning wakening, and her socialization was nil. Nothing in life was enjoyable for her, nothing done simply because it was fun. Her whole life was duty-bound, with fidelity to obligation her primary virtue.

The second evident condition was a terrible, all-pervasive sense of shame within her. She was obsessed with confidentiality, insisting that no one should know anything about her. She resisted all suggestions to share some of her issues in group therapy, and kept herself locked behind a wall of proprieties.

Of diagnostic significance was Theresa's obsessive-compulsive behavior, not only in her hoarding supplies, but in the overly rigid perfectionism that consumed her life. She had to be in absolute control of everything in order to sustain a minimal sense of security. So it took a while for me to establish enough of a relationship wherein she was able to let me inside the defensive structure around her.

Theresa's life story, although unique in its details, contained destructive themes experienced by too many people. She was born in Southern Germany, just before Hitler ascended to power, the oldest of five children in a farming family. Her father was a chronically unhappy man, who controlled the family by his seething temper. Outside the family he was seen as a jovial, friendly man, greeting all the villagers with a warm word of welcome. Inside the home he was morose, complaining, intolerant, demanding, and impatient.

Mother was a pious, quiet, socially inhibited woman, older than her husband, but totally dominated by him. She carried out her mothering role in a state of chronic fear lest she do something to upset her mean-tempered husband. Early in life, Theresa showed some of the compulsivity that was to arise so dramatically in her late adulthood. She had been responsible for certain household chores from a very young age, and she carried them out with obsessive perfection.

When Theresa was seven, the war began, and her father was called into the army. In spite of the economic hardship this imposed, life at home became much happier. There was even some laughter in the house, and it was the only time she remembered her mother smiling. It was hard for Theresa to admit that she secretly hoped her father would not return.

But he was discharged in 1941 just after his fifth child was born, sent home to care for his family. The dark pall fell over her life again. Father's moroseness was worse when he returned, and angry bitterness was his predominant mood. As the oldest child, Theresa felt overly responsible to save her family. When she was 11, she overheard a conversation between her mother and father where he threatened to commit suicide. It then became her self-appointed task to insure this did not happen, and she redoubled her efforts never to do anything to disappoint him in the hope of keeping him alive.

As the tide of the war turned against Germany, life became harder, and food, clothing, and fuel became scarce. They kept the farm, although they were forced to house German soldiers. Their livestock and crops were all taken to feed the military, and the family was barely able to keep themselves going. After the war, the family struggled to get back on its feet.

Theresa entered the convent at the age of 18, and over the next 35 years, returned home only three times. Although she told others about the wonderful parents she had and the ideal family she came from, she had no desire to go home for more regular visits. Her work became her life.

War does terrible things to people and some of its worst victims are found among the survivors. But it was not the war that caused Theresa's chronically unhappy life. Although that event framed her childhood, a far deeper cruelty robbed her of the joy that could have been hers.

Theresa had been sexually abused by her father. He had initiated the abuse when she was six, and it continued until she left home at age 18. Although never spoken of at home, it seems impossible that her mother could have been ignorant of what was going on, since her father regularly made nocturnal visits to Theresa's bed. Yet from the beginning, Theresa instinctually knew this was something that could never be talked about, not even with her mother.

As an adult in therapy, Theresa could finally begin to talk about her victimization. Her breakthrough occurred on the day after a group therapy session, where one of the members spoke about her own childhood sexual abuse. Although unable to speak in the group, the other woman's courage in speaking out prompted Theresa to look into her painful past. What she faced were not recovered memories, but rather, events so painfully vivid and surrounded with shame that she had not been able to acknowledge them to this time.

As Theresa recounted the violation experienced at the hands of her father, profound waves of grief and shame engulfed her. This man who was so puritanically strict with his family was doing the very things he condemned as evil. In the process, he was taking from her any sense of ownership of her own self. She was convinced there must be something innately bad about her if her father did these bad things to her. The healthy side of her wished her father dead; but this thought was so reprehensible that she denied it, and went to the other extreme of keeping him alive.

She also remembered incidents when the German soldiers living in their house and barn forced her to perform oral sex on them. Looking back, she realized her father was using her to placate the soldiers for food. She was sacrificed to keep the family going.

I often find myself wondering how people survive horrors such as those experienced by Theresa. That she survived as well as she did from extreme violative behavior and abusive indifference, from the very people on whom she should have been able to rely for safety and protection, is a wonder. Her father—and mother, by silent assent—took away Theresa's right to live her life as a search for her own happiness. Her only reason for living became to meet the needs of others. This was far worse than the physical violence done to her, worse than the loss of her childhood and its innocence.

The Way to Recovery

Theresa believed she kept her father alive (and her own rage at bay) by being perfect, but she was not perfect enough to make them all one big happy family. If only she was more perfect, all would be well. Becoming a nun was one way to be a "better person" and, at least in her perception, remove sex from her life. This same perfectionistic attitude was obvious in her work as a nurse. Although well respected and admired for her nursing skills, she had to be in absolute control in order for her to maintain perfection. This explained her hoarding behavior; no matter what crisis could possibly occur, she was prepared.

Much of her psychotherapy focused on recalling and re-experiencing the sexual, physical, and psychological trauma of her early life. Theresa began to understand the effects these had on her subsequent life, and saw how she was totally divorced from living in a personally satisfying way. She faced the rage that was pushed down deeply inside her, and was able to find some relief from it by expressing it in the safe context of the therapist's office.

Both the sharing of her shame-filled past and the insight into how it affected her gave Theresa a sense of freedom, a feeling that she could be the person she chose to be, rather than someone who lived to serve the needs of others. There was still one thing that needed to be done, however, in order for Theresa to be free of the crippling abuse; she needed to confront her father over what he did.

Her father was now an elderly man, living as a pensioner on the no longer active family farm, alone since his wife died five years ago. Age had mellowed him, and he lived for the visits of his children and grandchildren. In all their letters over these thirty-plus years, neither had mentioned what had occurred between them. Theresa worried about upsetting him and destroying the peace of his twilight years; but she also knew she would never be fully free of her burden until she talked about it with her father.

She made a decision to talk about the abuse by phone, then arrange a visit to Germany so they could face each other. During the first conversation, Theresa told her father of her psychotherapy, and remembrance of what he had done when she was a child. At first, her father was angry over her "accusations," and blamed the therapist for putting ideas into her head. Why was she trying to ruin his life now? "The past is the past, and best left alone," he shouted. She did not debate with him, but stuck to her guns, asking to understand why he did this to her. He hung up the phone.

A week later, Theresa phoned again. This time, he remonstrated that those were terrible times, life was difficult for all, and she did not know how hard it was for him to hold the family together. She listened, but went back to her point: He was her father, she was a little girl, and he violated her, destroying both her childhood and a major part of her personhood. Why had he done this? Again, he hung up on her, but phoned several days later and asked her to come visit.

Their meeting was a difficult and painful one. Amid tearful sobs, her father acknowledged what he had done and asked Theresa for forgiveness. She was not able to give that yet, but told him that despite everything that had happened, she did love him as her father and prayed that some day she could forgive. What she needed now was to understand.

Theresa and her father spent several days together, talking about those years. Her father listened as Theresa, as honestly and forthrightly as she could, spoke about what her past had been for her. Her father listened, sometimes defensively, but more often accepting. They visited her mother's grave together, and spent time with Theresa's brothers and sister. When they said farewell at the airport, both knew that they would never see each other again.

Theresa's therapy was not over yet. To this point, her religious vocation and selfless devotion to helping others provided the meaning and purpose in her life. This meaning was built on an escape from self; she was only "worthy" when she was a self-sacrificing nurse and nun. As she was able to reach a more self-centered sense of worth, knowing that she had a right to pursue her own fulfillment, the foundation of meaning in her religious calling crumbled. What was she going to do with her life?

We need to be selfish before we can become authentically altruistic. This is why we have adolescence, a time for self-liberation and self-discovery; we explore who we are and search for our own pathway into the future. If we lack this selfish era in our growth and become prematurely altruistic, our altruism is apt to be nothing more than disguised self-seeking. As paradoxical as it may seem, it is from this "selfishness" that we make the most significant contribution to the well-being of others.

Theresa's devotion to others arose not from a genuine concern for the poor and the suffering, but in response to her own sense of inner worthlessness. As contributory as this might have been, she was really using others to feel good about herself. When her own life became valuable to her in and of itself, the former focus of her efforts was lost.

Theresa had several options. She could return to the lay state, and support herself through nursing. Although she gave this serious consideration, she chose to remain within her religious order, as she saw there the potential for a fuller life. She further decided to study other healing arts besides traditional nursing, including massage, meditative practice, and movement therapy.

Theresa wanted to return to Central America, but to a different country. There, with new therapies (along with some unofficial psychotherapy), she would help religious and health care workers achieve more wellness in their own lives. She anticipated that this would be a satisfying thing to do, and she knew she would enjoy it.

If we want to hear those voices within ourselves which call us to new meaning in life, we must abandon the meaning and purpose of our early years. In this way, we permit ourselves to discover what really gives a sense of peace and worth to our existence. Life may or may not have an inherent meaning and purpose—this is up to the philosophers and theologians to debate. But it is up to each of us to unfold and create meaning in our lives from within our lived experience.

Questions for Discussion

1. Have you ever come face-to-face with the possibility that life may be meaningless? If so, what was the struggle like? What did you discover that gave your life meaning? What did you find in this chapter that will affect your search for meaning and purpose, or enhance the sense of meaning you may already have?

2. What in your life is more important to you than life itself; in other words, what would you die for? Is there a person for whom you would make the ultimate sacrifice? A principle? A value?

3. Have you been seduced by something that promised meaning, but later became burdensome and destructive to your spirituality? If so, what helped you escape and find a more life-giving meaning?

4. What has the potential to destroy spirituality for you? What deepens spirituality for you?

Chapter 14

The Final Word

Where do we stand now in our pursuit of wellness? The need for physical wellness is obvious; we take care of our bodies by doing what protects and sustains our physical health. Our commitment to following good physical health practices remains foundational, even though the actions we take toward good health may change with new discoveries. Striving for physical wellness is generally clear-cut and relatively easy.

Psychological wellness also demands that we take positive steps to sustain our psychological health. It is incumbent on each of us to consciously live our lives in psychologically healthy ways, following good mental health practices in our day-to-day living. And as we look to the medical healer to restore health when our bodies become diseased, so, too, we need look to healers of the psyche to help recover—or find—the sense of peace and satisfaction that arises from emotional health.

For most of us, the major challenge comes in our endeavor to find spiritual wellness. This may take more strength, courage, and ingenuity than either physical or psychological well-being. And although there are generally reliable guides to achieving physical and psychological wellness, this is not particularly true for spirituality. There are a number of spiritualities available to us, many of which are exploitive, feeding the affluence or power of their leaders rather than helping us develop our own spiritual nature. Examples abound of people who, in response to the call to self-transcendence, are led onto destructive pathways.

We become seduced into following those who offer to nourish our spiritual hunger through some "-ism," while ignoring our prophets, those who point the finger at false and misleading spiritual authorities. These very prophets are then vilified and destroyed by the people they are trying to warn. Institutionalized spiritualities proffer the answers, the truth, and insist on a unified affirmation that their propositions are the path to authentic spirituality. The temptation to assent is formidable, but full of risk.

I do not know how to guard against the destroyers of spirituality. Most people, however, in their intuitive perceptions, can recognize those who would lead us astray. We know that true spirituality arises out of deep personal experience, and not from the affirmation of dogmas or blind obedience to those who claim to possess the truth. Even when we succumb to the sense of security that authority offers, human sense eventually prevails and we return to the wonder-filled search for truth. With novelist and poet André Gide, we "believe those who are seeking the truth, but doubt those who find it."

In addition to the external threats to our search for an authentic spirituality, there are threats inside each of us which menace our efforts. One of these is the drive to find our moral and spiritual truth in individualistic isolation. As we fail to thrive physically or psychologically when we lack connectedness with other people, so, too, we fail to thrive spiritually when we remove ourselves from community. Community protects against the lure of idiosyncratic thinking.

Each of us needs interactive reaction to our perceptions of what it means to be a moral person; the possibility of making our morals synonymous with what pleases us or profits us is too great. The same danger threatens our spiritual search, if conducted apart from interactive relationships. Whether the community that we bond with is a religious organization, a faith community, or an informal group of truth seekers, the critical response from a group of others protects us against self-delusion.

Narcissism is another major hindrance to the construction of a spirituality, and to the building of a moral code. (This condition is more fully defined in Chapter 2.) Although narcissism can interfere with our psychological well-being by limiting our capacity to surrender into a loving relationship, spiritual growth is possible only to the degree that we move beyond narcissism, since spirituality builds on self-transcendence. This is true for both primary narcissism, which we are born with, and secondary narcissism, which can develop as we work toward an altruism grounded in empathy.

It is worth repeating that there is some degree of narcissism in all of us. Narcissism always suggests some defect in our empathetic capability, an inability to put ourselves "in another's shoes" and feel what the other is feeling. In fact, empathy is the antidote to narcissism, and human nature is such that we exist with an admixture of both. But the degree to which we can keep our narcissistic tendencies to a minimum, and thus permit our empathetic response to grow, is the degree to which we move further into maturity.

The narcissistic wounds that arise when we do fail in something or are defeated in our drive to achieve can be growth opportunities for us. They can provide the chance to confront our wounded self-esteem, see it for what it is, and reconsider the values we strive for leading, hopefully, to spiritual growth.

Our struggle should be to resist the temptation toward narcissistic solutions, opting instead for achieving greater authenticity in our lives. Actually, each of the "tasks" of wellness, including physical and psychological wellness, lead toward this goal because they bring us greater self-respect, more honesty with self and others, increased awareness of our own vulnerability, and strength found more in truth than in illusions.

From my experience as a psychotherapist, there are two paths that seekers of truth pursue; either path seems to bring them to a more authentic sense of personhood. Also, it appears to me that people following either path achieve a deeper level of spirituality in their lives and find a sense of peace. This is so even though the paths are divergent, and bring seekers to different, even contradictory, places.

The first, perhaps the minority, live without illusions in a life circumscribed by birth and death, believing in nothing before and nothing after. They live in awareness of an essential personal isolation, while reaching for meaningful human encounters that provide the joy of companionship. They accept life as their responsibility, and they recognize that what they make of serendipitous events is within their power.

Although they know that they cannot change destiny, they can make the most of it.

These people do not look for transcendent meaning to human existence. They take satisfaction in what they can do today, like making another's life richer, protecting the environment for the generations to come, saving a life, relieving someone's suffering, or working against oppression. Their essential purpose is that their life means something to someone else.

They live their life aware of a connection to others, and with a sense of responsibility toward them and their shared environment. They do not yearn to discover God, or seek a relational connection to the divine. They have, in theologian Paul Tillich's phrase, "the courage to be" in the face of meaninglessness, aloneness, freedom, and death. Living in this courage brings a sense of peace.

The second pathway proceeds somewhat differently. It may start when mortality is brought into sharper focus, or we feel the aloneness from the loss of a relationship, or an event forces us to reevaluate life's meaning. It is often preceded by a bout of depression, a time of confusion, or an event that shakes our self-image to its foundation. This crisis is the invitation to undertake the journey into self-discovery.

Some will reject the invitation, grasping on to the familiar until the crisis passes. The crack in their psychic defense opened by the crisis gets sealed over, the anxiety buried, and they go back to merely surviving, finding fun wherever they can. But in choosing this route, an opportunity was missed; the crisis did not bring them to a new life awareness.

Other people, however, refuse to anesthetize the dread and take seriously the questions raised in a crisis. They put aside the illusions and become seekers. They find God, or at least, God takes on a new meaning in their life. It may be more accurate, however, to say that God finds them. Now they have moved to a place inhabited by the Divine, with an openness to understand what their life is about, and a willingness to push aside limiting preconceptions.

This path encompasses many of the same characteristics found along the path of the non-theist; but it is framed by a belief in meaning beyond the bonds of time and place. Religions and myths tell us that the Divine Presence is more often found in fears than in complacencies, in crises than in triumphs, in moments of focus rather than in distractions. Even if an awareness of this Divine Presence is not immediate, a crisis forces a reevaluation of life's purpose, and leads to a view framed broader than mere self-seeking.

Perhaps it is just this movement from self that places us in God's path. All religions also teach that God is more often found among the poor than among the rich, among the powerless than among the powerful, with the questioners than among the knowers, with the sinners than among the saved. Could it be that in placing ourselves amidst the poor, the powerless, the questioners, and the sinners we are in a place where God can find us?

Whenever a spiritually transformative process takes place, illusions about life and death, meaning and value, freedom and responsibility, isolation and relatedness, self-focus and other-directedness, are stripped away. The comfort of the reassuring answers are abandoned, and one stands before God— or life, or fate—naked and empty, stripped of superficiality and pretensions. It is then that God can become known to us. This is not without risk. We may find that we receive no reassurance of divine support, only silent emptiness. Yet even this allows us to live our lives with a sense of uncompromised integrity. Further, who knows what revelation will come tomorrow?

A better understanding of how God comes into our lives can be found in the work of two different people, one a theologian, the other, a psychologist. The lives of both illustrate the search for an authentic spirituality, and show the effects of the human struggle that each of us, man or woman, goes through.

A Life in Grace

Paul Tillich, arguably the preeminent theological thinker of the twentieth century—some believe the most "dangerous theologian" of any century—lived a personal life that was apparently in marked contrast to what one expects from such a God-centered person. He reached for an understanding of the Infinite, breaking the bonds of his Evangelical Lutheran background in his efforts to apprehend the eternal with uncompromising personal integrity.

Tillich was a deeply tormented man, often depressed and anxious, with a self-described demonic side which often led him into despair. He was born in Prussia in the last third of the nineteenth century, and died close to the start of the last third of the twentieth, effectively bridging two centuries. Ordained in 1912 into the Lutheran church, he married early to a woman older than himself.

While serving as a chaplain in the German army in World War I, he suffered two nervous breakdowns, and eventually returned home to find his wife pregnant by his best friend. He stayed with her through the birth of the child to protect them from social stigma, then left and began an academic career, teaching in some of the major universities of Germany. Recognized for both his brilliance and originality, he became a major theological force in post-war Europe. An early and vigorous opponent of the Nazi movement, he was expelled from the University of Frankfurt in 1933, the first Christian to be so treated by the Nazis when they came to power.

He emigrated to the United States with his second wife and their child, and accepted a teaching post at Union Theological Seminary in New York, where he spent the majority of his academic career as professor of both systematic theology and the philosophy of religion. He also held chairs at Harvard, the University of Chicago, and Yale, among others, and was highly respected as a teacher and preacher, theologian and philosopher.

All the while his personal life was deeply troubled. Much to the pain of his wife, Hannah, marriage was not able to contain Tillich's sexual expressiveness. He had numerous romantic relationships with women, some of whom were students, and some with whom he had a pastoral relationship. By the standards of the 1990s, he would be judged a sexual predator, one who violated his professional responsibilities, and whose ethical and moral behavior would be of legal concern.

Tillich himself was tortured by his behavior, distressed over his sexual compulsivity and inability to be faithful to his marital commitment. His attempts to justify his "immorality" ultimately added to his depression, and he lived his life a tormented individual.

None of this detracts from the powerful insights he gave us concerning the human struggle to confront the ultimate concerns of life. His book, *The Courage to Be,* is, I believe, a major contribution to our understanding of human spirituality. I would like to quote an excerpt from a sermon Tillich gave in St. Paul's Chapel at Columbia University, on the occasion of his sixtieth birthday. It captures well the ability to seek truth in our lives, and surrender to the divine activity in our spirit.

Grace strikes us when we are in great pain and restlessness. It strikes us when we walk through the dark valley of a meaningless and empty life. It strikes us when we feel that our separation is deeper than usual, because we feel we have violated another life, a life which we have loved, or from which we were estranged. It strikes us when our disgust for our own being, our indifference, our weakness, our hostility, and our lack of direction and composure have become intolerable to us. It strikes us when, year after year, the longed-for perfection of life does not appear, when the old compulsions reign within us as they have for decades, when despair destroys all joy and courage.

Sometimes at that moment a wave of light breaks into our darkness, and it is as though a voice were saying: "You are accepted, accepted by that which is greater than you, and the name of which you do not know." Do not ask for the name now; perhaps you will find it later. Do not try to do anything now; perhaps later you will do much. Do not seek for anything; do not perform anything; do not intend anything. Simply accept the fact that you are accepted!

(The Shaking of the Foundation, NY:
Charles Scribner & Sons, 1948.)

Paul Tillich did not believe in God as a separate being, but rather as Being itself. This led some to label him, incorrectly, as an "atheist" or "pantheist." Nor did he believe in a personal immortality. He found the courage to be, lacking the consolation of a personal God and a belief in the afterlife, living with the reality of the universe as he perceived it and as the Divine intended it. He found relief from his personal struggle in this acceptance, and in the acceptance he experienced from God.

A Life Well-Lived

I know much less about C. Gilbert Wrenn than I know about Tillich. I once met Wrenn, but only to shake hands and exchange a few words of conversation. He struck me as a gentle, kind man who seemed to sincerely care for other people. As testimony to the esteem his professional colleagues held for him, the Gilbert and Kathleen Wrenn Award for a Humanitarian and Caring Person was established by the American Counseling Association.

Wrenn was born in 1902 and, to the best of my knowledge, is still living an active life at this writing. He has spent a lifetime as a teacher, counselor, psychotherapist, and consultant, and is Professor Emeritus of Counseling Psychology at Arizona State University. Although I know nothing of his religious beliefs, he strikes me as a man of deep spirituality. He has written numerous books and articles; the following quote is from a personal reflection published shortly after he retired from Arizona State University. It is, without doubt, the most popular of all his writings, quoted more often than his more scholarly books and articles.

Does it seem bizarre to you that I, at age 73, have a future? Currently I talk to groups, attend boards and commissions, write, listen to others, love others. This is what I have been doing all my life. I have an endearing wife, who looks after me beautifully and gives love and service to many others while maintaining her own remarkable stature among people. She, too, is doing what she has done with me for the past forty-nine years.

Someday, soon perhaps, some ailment will attack my body and it will be unable to fight back hard enough. I, as I am known to others, will have ceased to exist. Some people who love me deeply—my family, perhaps one or two others—will keep the image of me alive and vibrant, but for most I will have become a rather vague memory, a loving memory, I hope, but only that. Is there a future for me beyond the time when the energy of my physical self is stifled and my body becomes ashes?

I think there is a future for me. I do not fear Death, for it affects only the death of my body. Of course, I may panic when Death knocks on my door, but as of now I see Death as introducing me to a new adventure. Life in my present state of existence has always been an adventure—loving, seeking, finding fulfillment in part and then finding new goals to beckon me on. After the death of my body, the excitement will surely not be done; it may increase. I take with me into my new existence all that I have become, and I will perhaps find a freer chance to become even more.

Of course, I know nothing of this life-beyond-the-body, but I have no fear of it, only a tingling anticipation.... I have heard... that one lives on and on and on in the lives of people one has touched and that this is immortality. I accept this, but it is not enough for me. If the energy of this physical universe is never lost but only changes form, why not the same for the psychic energy of "me"?

It has always seemed inconceivable to me that all that is built into a person should disappear with the stopping of a heart. If our Creator conserves energy in the physical world, He would surely do so in the spiritual.... Perhaps the spirit, the "person" part of me, has always lived, has been passed on from expression to expression of me over the millennia. This is an awesome thought, to be sure, but no more so than the mystery of our complex selves existing in the here and now.

Death, I do not fear you, but neither do I want you. I

love too much of this life, and I love too many people. There will be anguish and longing for this life and these people—just before you lead me "somewhere." But with all of the love and beauty here, surely there will be even more "there." I trust you, Death. You are not my friend, but neither are you my enemy.

Perhaps Victor Hugo said it better: "When I go down to the grave, I can say like many others—I have finished my day's work—but I cannot say—I have finished my life. My day's work will begin the next morning. The tomb is not a blind alley, it is a thoroughfare. It closes on the twilight; it opens on the dawn."

("The Future of a Person—Me." *The Personnel and Guidance Journal,* Vol. 54, No. 1, September 1975.)

Let us return to Paul Tillich who can, I believe, bring us a step closer to understanding spirituality, albeit deeply rooted in his Christian heritage. It summarizes the stance that I have observed time and again in those who, Prometheus-like, soar in intensity to a life lived in the spirit, finding peace even amid the pain and suffering, joy and pleasure that being human is filled with.

Nothing is demanded of you—no idea of God, and no goodness in yourself, not your being religious, not your being Christian, not your being wise, and not your being moral. But what is demanded is only your being open and willing to accept what is given to you, the New Being, the Being of love and justice and truth, as it is manifest in Him Whose yoke is easy and Whose burden is light.

(*The Shaking of the Foundations,* NY:
Charles Scribners & Sons, 1948.)

In the pages of this book, I have reflected on the lives of several people whom I would label "healthy." All found a sense of peace within their lives, along with personal ownership and responsibility. Each had pain, moments of great sadness, disappointments, and failures, as well. These, too, became part of the fabric of their life, contributing to the person they came to be. And, is not the whole purpose of life what we become?

If we were the engineers of our own lives, planning them out from the beginning, the plan would be much different from the reality. All of us, in looking forward, would make events happen differently than they actually do. But, in looking back, it is the well person who would not make events happen differently. Even the losses and deaths, failures and disappointments, are indispensable to fully becoming who we are.

Wellness is the commitment to live our lives in a way that is responsible to our bodies, our minds, and our spirits. It is also our responsibility to accept whatever fate—or God—hands to us, using this to create a life that brings us a sense of peace and happiness. This is what wellness is all about.

Questions for Discussion

1. Who in your life keeps you honest in your pursuit of integrity and authenticity? What protects you from narcissistic self-delusion? What community do you call "home"?

2. What narcissistic traits do you see in your personality? What altruistic traits are also there? Do others confirm or deny these narcissistic and altruistic traits? Where and by whom is your true self most affirmed?

3. This chapter speaks of two divergent paths that truth-seekers take in their pursuit of the spiritual. One finds self-transcendence in the here-and-now world of immanence; the other, in a transcendent Being or purposefulness. Which pathway have you taken? Can you understand the other path? Are you still seeking?

4. Having read this book, what does wellness now mean to you? What positive actions will you take to express your commitment to wellness, and fully incorporate a healthy attitude into your life?

Suggested Readings

Benner, D., *Psychotherapy and the Spiritual Quest*. Grand Rapids, MI: Baker Book House, 1988.

Fowler, J., *Stages of Faith: The Psychology of Human Development and the Quest for Meaning*. San Francisco: Harper & Row, 1981.

Groeschel, B.J., *Spiritual Passages: The Psychology of Spiritual Development*. New York: Crossroad Books, 1983.

Kahoe, R. and Meadow, M., *Psychology of Religion: Religion in Individual Lives*. New York: Harper & Row, 1984.

Kohlberg, L., *The Psychology of Moral Development*. New York: Harper & Row, 1984.

Levenson, E., *The Ambiguity of Change*. New York: Basic Books, 1983.

Lidz, T., *The Person: His & Her Development Throughout the Life Cycle*. New York: Basic Books, 1983.

Pelikan, J., *The World Treasury of Modern Religious Thought*. Boston: Little, Brown, 1990.

Rogers, C., *On Becoming A Person*. Boston: Houghton Mifflin, 1961.

Szasz, T., *The Myth of Psychotherapy: Mental Healing as Religion, Phetonic, and Repression*. New York: Syracuse University Press, 1988.

Tyrrell, T., *Urgent Longings*. Mystic, CT: Twenty-Third Publications, 1994.

Of Related Interest...

Healing Wounded Emotions
Overcoming Life's Hurts
Martin Padovani
Describes how our emotional and spiritual lives interact, and challenges readers to live fuller, more satisfying lives.
0-89622-333-7, 128 pp, $6.95 (order W-22)
Audiobook: Three 60-minute cassettes, $24.95 (order A-44)

The Work Trap
Rediscovering Leisure, Redefining Work
Martin C. Helldorfer
Discover how to ease work addiction and work-fixation and move beyond "busyness" in order to become truly involved in both work and personal activities.
0-89622-638-7, 128 pp, $9.95 (order M-31)

Urgent Longings
Reflections on Infatuation, Intimacy and Sublime Love
Thomas J. Tyrrell
This book reveals the experience of infatuation, and its attendant pain and suffering as a natural, normal part of human growth and development.
0-89622-573-9, 96 pp, $7.95 (order W-65)

The Adventure of Intimacy
A Journey Through Broken Circles
Thomas J. Tyrrell
The author uses the story of his grandparents as a framework for studying intimacy. He shows how natural forces, as well as individual personalities, affected their relationships in life and the role that faith played.
0-89622-532-1, 128 pp, $7.95 (order C-93)

Available at religious bookstores or from:

TWENTY-THIRD PUBLICATIONS
XXIII P.O. Box 180, Mystic, CT 06355

To order or request a free catalog of other quality books and video call
1-800-321-0411